SEX AND YOUNG PEOPLE

THE KNOWLEDGE TO GUIDE THE TEENAGER IN YOUR LIFE

First published in 2001 by Mercier Press
5, French Church Street, Cork
Tel (021) 4275040; Fax (021) 4274969
E.mail: books@mercier.ie

16 Hume Street, Dublin 2
Tel (01) 661 5299; Fax (01) 661 8583
E.mail: books@marino.ie

Trade enquiries to CMD Distribution
55A Spruce Avenue
Stillorgan Industrial Park
Blackrock, County Dublin
Tel: (01) 294 2556; Fax: (01)294 2564
E.mail:cmd@columba.ie

© Carmel Wynne 2001

ISBN 1 85635 358 3

10 9 8 7 6 5 4 3 2 1

A CIP record for this title is available from the British Library

Cover design by Penhouse Design

Printed in Ireland by ColourBooks, Baldoyle Industrial Estate, Dublin 13

This book is sold subject to the condition that it shall not, by way of trade or otherwise, be lent, resold, hired out or otherwise circulated without the publisher's prior consent in any form of binding or cover other than that in which it is published and without a similar condition including this condition being imposed on the subsequent purchaser.

No part of this publication may be reproduced or transmitted in any form or by any means, electronic or mechanical, including photocopying, recording or any information or retrieval system, without the prior permission of the publisher in writing.

Sex and Young People

The Knowledge to Guide the Teenager in Your Life

Carmel Wynne

Mercier Press

*This book is dedicated to Colm with lots of love and appreciation. Greater love than this no husband has than to proofread and offer to undertake the tedious and tiresome job of making amendments to his wife's book. Your loving support is deeply appreciated.
Thank you.*

Acknowledgements

So many people have contributed directly, indirectly and unknowingly to this book. I want to thank the many students and teachers who made such helpful suggestions about the contents and who shared stories and case histories. Their names have been altered but their voices echo through the chapters.

Thank you to Jo O'Donoghue and Jane Casey in Mercier Press who edited this work. I also want to thank my husband Colm, who made their job easier by proof-reading many drafts of this work before they saw it. I am so grateful for his support, encouragement and especially his understanding on the many occasions when there was no dinner because I was writing.

I am deeply grateful to my daughters for their ongoing love and support. Aileen, Niamh, Deirdre Anne and Aoife Marie, thank you for being great daughters. I am so proud that you have grown into such lovely young women and that Aoife Marie is such a great hugger. Welcome to John Wynne and James Robinson, who are marrying into the family, and to Lynne Petrie, whom we introduce as our adopted daughter.

My thanks are also due to John Callanan SJ for his suggestions and support during the writing and editing of this book. Many other friends supported me too – Aidan and Joyce O'Hara, Gay Waterstone, Joy Conville and the Tabor community. I especially want to thank Mary Kavanagh and David Weakliam O. Carm, two special friends who are so wonderfully supportive when I need them. Your acceptance and love are a great blessing to me and are gifts that I treasure.

Thank you all.

Contents

	Introduction	7
1	How Do You Know If You're Ready for Sex?	15
2	Looking for Romance	30
3	Early Sexual Pressure	48
4	Understanding Peer Pressure	62
5	So The Earth Moved!	79
6	Performance Anxiety	92
7	Six in the Bed – and It's Not an Orgy!	106
8	Contraception	123
9	Sexually Transmitted Diseases	141
10	Straight Talking about Coming Out	155
11	Finding Your Dream Partner	175
12	Your Sacred Self	197
	Bibliography	221

INTRODUCTION

FOR PARENTS AND TEACHERS

Over the last two years I have had requests from many parents and teachers to write a book for teenagers that will encourage them to make sexually responsible decisions. 'Sexual responsibility' is part of the modern jargon that is widely used. Yet when people are asked, 'What specifically do you mean by "sexually responsible decisions"?' there are great differences in the replies.

Many parents appear to believe that all young people are having sex, and that learning about being sexually responsible simply means being educated about 'safe sex' practices. Others think that only a minority of teenagers are sexually active: even these people hold contradictory views. Some appear to think that only young people who are madly in love have sex, while others hold the opposite view, believing that modern young people are so casual about sex that they are all having one-night stands. Few are aware that 'safe sex' practices do not fully protect against virally transmitted diseases like genital warts and genital herpes.

Some parents want young people to have clear, accurate information about enjoying healthy relationships but fail to take account of the fact that a teenager's view of a healthy relationship may be wildly different from an adult's. Few adults have the communication skills to teach young people that they can set limits, and that it is sexually responsible to be honest about what one does and does not want to do with a partner. Many tell me that they themselves need to learn how to do this with their own spouse or partner.

Only a tiny number of teenagers are happy about how they were educated about the more sensitive issues, like contraception, sexually transmitted diseases and homosexuality. Such poor education is grossly irresponsible, because sexual ignorance, which is the lack of correct information, puts young lives at risk. Many parents who suspect that teenagers are sexually active are terrified about pregnancy and unaware of the risks of STDs. There is a higher risk of sexually active young people picking up a sexual disease than there is of their being party to a pregnancy.

There is no denying that there is enormous peer pressure on our young people to have sex. The days when a mother or father could forbid premarital sex are long gone. Laying down the law simply does not work in this day and age. Television is the new sex educator and adolescents are influenced by the way that teenage lovers are portrayed on the screen. Premarital sex is becoming the norm.

Sex education programmes which only give information about sex and contraception have little impact on changing behaviour. Helping young people to work out for themselves the consequences of behaviour that they consider to be acceptable challenges them to think differently. When they have an understanding of how they are affected by their erupting hormones, peer pressure and their own powerful sex drive, it's amazing how quickly they can come up with insights into better ways to deal with their feelings.

This book encourages young people to challenge the popular belief that feeling ready or being in love makes it OK to have sex. It examines the myths about romance and clearly explains how to deal with sexual pressure and performance anxiety. It encourages young people to enjoy their heightened sexual awareness and educates them about the risks of engaging in sexual activity with anyone who has had previous sexual partners. It challenges the assumption that a virgin is someone who has not had intercourse and explains that the sexual intimacy popularly known as 'fooling around' is high-risk behaviour.

Many sexually active young people talk as if they attain the heights of ecstasy in every encounter. Their peers are not sure whether or not they are lying, but not to be outdone, they also exaggerate about how the earth moved for them too. This creates pressure about sexual performance that previous generations did not experience to the same extent. Chapter 6 brings this performance anxiety out into the open and explains that people who find it necessary to talk about their sex life usually exaggerate because they are trying to prove something to themselves.

There are at least twice as many gay students in schools as there are gifted students. Many are bullied and have to cope with intolerant attitudes that make them feel isolated because of their difference. This affects every aspect of their lives and can seriously interfere with their studies. This book helps all young people, gay and straight, to understand their feelings and accept who they are. Family influences on relationships are dealt with in a sensitive, thought-provoking way. There is detailed information on the different kinds of contraception and clear warnings about the risks of contracting a sexual disease.

In the final chapters, 'Finding Your Dream Partner' and 'Your Sacred Self', the reader will discover that he or she is never dependent on anyone to meet their intimacy needs. Once young people have this awareness, they will find it easier to refuse to allow anyone to use them as a sexual object. That is what people are doing when they have a 'snog' before they have even exchanged names. Teenagers and young adults need to be aware that they deserve better than that, and in these chapters, they will learn that when they tell themselves, 'I deserve the best', even though they may not yet believe it to be true, their attitude will change and people will treat them better.

For Teenagers and Young Adults

I hope this book will help you to make decisions that will bring happiness, joy and fulfilment into your life in abundance. If you do not feel special and loved in a relationship, walk away. It's not a healthy relationship for you. If your boyfriend or girlfriend treats you better when you are on your own together than when they are with friends, don't stick around for the slagging. You deserve better.

I want you to set out to have the relationship you dream of, and not to settle for less. Trust me, it is better to be without a boyfriend or girlfriend than to be with someone who makes you feel miserable and insecure most of the time. When you allow yourself to be treated with disrespect, you damage your own self-esteem. This takes away your self-confidence. When you don't value yourself enough to say, 'This is not acceptable', your behaviour is giving your partner a message. We train people in the way they treat us.

When you settle for less than your dream, you will always feel cheated. You will live with a dissatisfaction that breeds regret. You will never be truly happy if you have the sense that there is something missing from your life that you could have had. Set goals. Follow your dream.

Do yourself a favour – read this book. If you want to enjoy sex that makes you feel loved and special, you need to feel comfortable with your partner. If you can't talk freely, you are not even ready to engage in foreplay. If you are not aware that talking is the first step in successful foreplay for women, stop! If you are not clear about the difference in male and female sexual responsiveness, you have a lot to learn.

Read on. You may be surprised at what you find. Discover that the belief most people have that sex is all about what happens in the genitals is way off the mark. Your brain, your thinking, your spiritual understanding and your emotional involvement play a far more important part in whether you enjoy sex than any techniques or sexual experiences that either you or your partner may have practised. If the relationship is not right, the sex can't be great.

Ignore what others tell you about the earth moving. People who know don't say, and those who say don't know.

1

How Do You Know If You're Ready For Sex?

Shane's Story

'Love is such a big deal for my girlfriend, Gina,' an embarrassed and confused Shane said. 'She's always snuggling up to me in public and wanting to hold my hand. She doesn't mind who's around. She's always telling me she loves me and if I'm late or do anything that upsets her, she gets so weepy that I feel guilty. As soon as anything goes wrong, she says: "You don't love me." When I do something nice for her, she is convinced that I love her, but if I'm in a bad mood she assumes that I don't love her. Her friends go on the same way. They are always talking about who is in love and what couples are fooling around and breaking up. Gina even wants me to get involved and tell her about the love lives of the students in my year. She expects me to know if Freddie is really serious about Sadie or if he's leading her on. I haven't a clue, but if I tell her I don't, she thinks I'm heartless and that I don't care. I don't know if I love her or not. She's really sexy and I fancy her a lot. I want to have sex with her but all this love stuff is doing my head in. I'm not sure that I'm ready for the kind of relationship that she wants.'

Gina's Story

'I really love Shane. I've been going out with him for nearly a month and he's really fun. He's the sexiest-looking boy around. We see each other almost every day and it's really cool. I know he loves me by the way he kisses me and when we fool around, but he's too shy to tell me. He's even shy about holding hands. All my friends say that he's crazy for me.

'He's my first real boyfriend, and even though I really love him, he's going too fast. He wants to have sex with me and I'm not sure that I'm ready. Having sex is a really big decision. I'm not Shane's first girlfriend. He was with my friend's cousin for nearly four months, and another friend, Sadie, told me that her brother said he knows other girls Shane had been with and she said that some of that crowd have genital warts. I'm not sure what they are, but I wouldn't give her the satisfaction of asking. I think she fancies Shane herself – maybe she said that to scare me off.

'I'm really scared to have sex. My mum would kill me if I got pregnant. But I'm afraid that if I say no, Shane will go off with someone else. I know loads of girls who'd have him and who couldn't care less whether he had warts or not. One part of me feels I'm ready for sex. I look very grown up – more like twenty than seventeen – and I'd love to know what it feels like. To tell the truth, I'm a bit embarrassed at still being a virgin because most of my friends say they've done it. Yet I'm afraid that if I do have sex, Shane will tell his friend Freddie, and he'll tell my brother, and everyone will find out.'

FEELING READY IS NOT A GOOD ENOUGH REASON

Once hormonal activity begins at puberty – and that can be as young as ten or eleven for a girl and a year or two later for a boy – it is perfectly natural to be curious about sex, to wonder what it feels like. The physical desire to have sex is there years before a person has the emotional maturity to deal with those powerful sexual feelings. It is only common sense to suggest that feeling ready is not a good enough reason to act on those feelings and have intercourse.

Losing your virginity is a really important decision. You never feel the same after you have been sexually intimate with a person. Something in you feels different, and for young people who have sex too soon, it's not a good feeling. Adolescent sex is rarely a mutually happy experience. It's not sexist to say that girls and boys think very differently about having sex. In general, girls have sex in order to get love. Boys used to give love in order to get sex, but that appears to be changing. In a recent British survey involving 1,000 teenagers from across all social classes, only 15 per cent of the boys gave love as the reason for having sex. In Holland, where having a relationship is important, 56 per cent of boys quoted love as a reason.

It's clearly risky for a woman to make a decision about being sexually intimate when the man is not interested in commitment. A girl or woman who is madly in love may be tempted to have sex. The myth that a man is more likely to fall in love after sex needs to be shattered. Women of all ages who have made this mistake say very similar things. They regret it the next day. They feel bad about themselves, and feel hurt at being used by a man who is not interested in a relationship beyond sex.

Feelings of rejection are emotionally damaging and get in the way of developing trust in future relationships.

When anyone tells me they are 'in love' and 'fancy the pants off' someone, I know immediately that it's not love they're talking about. I have no doubt that they believe that what they are saying is true. From their perspective, they *are* in love, but what they are talking about is powerfully strong sexual desire. Another word for this is plain and simple lust! It's interesting that while girls talk about being in love, boys discuss sex and how to get into a girl's knickers. They rarely mention love.

There isn't a great deal of difference between the twelve-year-old girl who sends her friends to set her up with the guy she fancies and the twenty-two-year-old single girl or newly separated woman who has her friend give a party, inviting the eligible man she finds attractive. People who find it hard to ask for what they want don't really change. They just get that little bit more sophisticated as they get older.

ONE-NIGHT STANDS

Today, almost a third of teenagers lose their virginity on a one-night stand. Alcohol is usually involved. It's a drug that lowers inhibitions and gives a false sense of self-confidence. Generally, it is unwise to make decisions based solely on sexual feelings. Before you agree to have sex, you need to think about what will happen afterwards. It sounds as if I'm taking all the romance out of it, but consider how romantic it is when two people have sex when they are drunk. Often, the truth is that they both know if they had been sober, they wouldn't have done it.

Sober, they simply couldn't have moved from first base.

How do you think a person who has sex feels when a partner doesn't want to see him or her again after they have had sex? Most teenage girls think it won't happen to them, and at least a third of them are wrong. A small number of young women are now behaving in a masculine way. They use males sexually and abandon them. It's not only teenagers who don't have the freedom to assert themselves sexually in healthy and loving ways. This is also true of adults who don't have a strong sense of self-esteem. Young people who don't have a lot of self-confidence are uncomfortable with their sexual desires and are unable to talk honestly about what they do and don't want to do sexually. As adults, there is rarely any marked improvement, because the skills needed to communicate about sexual wants and needs are never learned.

TRUST AND COMMITMENT

One reason why men and women find it hard to trust the other sex is because of incorrect information. People generalise about how the other sex thinks. It's amazing how many women still believe that men are only out for one thing – sex. While this is true of some, it is certainly not true of all men. There is a widespread belief that women want commitment from a man. Again, that is true for a lot of women – there are some girls who are already selecting names for their children while the man is deciding whether to ask for a third date. It is equally true that the last thing in the world other women want is to settle down and commit to one guy.

If you or I don't have the confidence to be open and

ask for what we want, or share how we feel, our partner cannot trust us. If I'm afraid to tell you honestly how I feel – in other words, if I lie to keep you comfortable – it's a clear sign that I don't feel secure in our relationship. My motives may be deeply caring and protective. I may be afraid of hurting your feelings or causing you pain; I may desire to protect you from information that would upset you. No matter how good my motives for dishonesty, the fact is that when I am not totally honest with another person, my behaviour is clearly saying, 'There is a lack of trust in this relationship'. I may say loving words, but they don't conceal the behaviour that shows I'm insecure and not free to be myself. When trust is lacking, so also is freedom.

There are always unresolved control issues when a person feels insecure. When I try to hide the part of myself that I fear you won't like, it's as if I put on a mask and act a role to conceal it. When I conceal any part of me, I have to pretend to be someone I am not. My intention may be to protect our relationship, yet hiding behind that mask harms me because I disempower myself. If I change my behaviour to keep you sweet, you have the power to control me. You may not be aware of what is going on, but I feel manipulated when I let you control me. People don't set out consciously to disrespect the other person, but when they manipulate situations, isn't that what they do? It not only takes courage, strength and sensitivity to overcome insecurity, it also takes honest communication.

Most of us grow up in families that fail to encourage us to speak out about our needs and desires. One result of this is that as adults, we are afraid to ask to have our needs met. We find it easier to manipulate others than to make a request. The tragedy is that we are unaware of what we are doing. If you don't know how to ask for what you want in a relationship, you are not yet ready for commitment.

It's obvious that if you or I don't have the freedom to discuss honestly what we want from a partner, we don't have the kind of intimate relationship or loving communication that leads to good sex. This is true whether one is married or single. If you don't feel free to talk openly with your partner, make a good decision. Learn to communicate.

If you are unmarried and don't feel able to talk about contraception and what will happen if it fails, you are definitely not ready to have sex. Even after you can freely discuss fertility control, a more sensitive topic to be aware of is your partner's sexual history. Sexual health is an issue that can no longer be ignored by sexually active people who may have contracted a disease from previous sexual partners.

Psychologists tell us that a great deal of teenage sex happens because the way many young people meet their need for affection is through sexual intimacy. It's not seen as macho for a young lad to ask for a hug, yet there is a widespread acceptance that boys will be boys and look for sex.

How Do Teenagers Know They're Ready?

'How do you know if you are ready for sex?' is not as simple a question as it may at first appear. The popular answers – 'Wait until you're the legal age' or 'Wait until you feel ready' – are simply not good enough. It's well known that teen sex is rarely a good experience, because young boys know little about foreplay and ejaculate quickly. Teenage girls usually have romantic expectations that are not fulfilled. They expect to feel loved and special, but frequently they end up feeling used and rejected. I will discuss this more in Chapter 4, 'Understanding Peer Pressure'. It is not so widely accepted that large numbers of married women have lost interest in sex because their partners fail to give them a sense of being loved and valued.

When older teenagers are asked about their first sexual experience, the word that comes up time and time again is regret. Over a third of young people believe that they had sex too soon and regret that they didn't wait. The younger adolescents were when they first had intercourse, the more likely they are to express regret. The primary biological purpose of sex is to make babies. Here is a tough question. How long do you think it takes from the time a baby is born until the child is in a position to care financially for himself or herself? If contraception fails and you are involved in a pregnancy, that's how long the two of you will have a child who depends on you.

Readiness for sex depends on a mature understanding of the legal position, the family values you hold, religious considerations and how influenced you are by peer pressure. The expectations you have about love and what men and women want from a relationship, and whether you can distinguish between loving and lustful feelings all have a bearing on how ready you are. This generation of teenagers has watched countless couples on television and in films screaming with passion in the throes of sexual ecstasy. They wrongly assume that the louder the passionate screams, the more satisfying the sex. Before you agree to have sex, here are a few questions that you should think about. If you got your sex education from friends or the media, you can't trust what you believe. To base a decision to have sex on what your friends say is sheer madness.

Do you know the legal penalties for engaging in underage sex? Have you considered the possibility of parenthood, or the risks of infection with a sexually transmitted disease? If you can't talk about protection, you're not ready. You won't be ready until you have the maturity to be sensitive to your own feelings, expectations and values and have the communication skills to share them with your partner. Feeling ready is never a good enough reason. You are a sexual person, so from the time you reach puberty, you will be aware of having sexual feelings. Those feelings will create powerful sexual desires in you. This is normal and healthy, but it is not healthy to use the feeling of being ready as the sole criterion for making a decision about your sexual behaviour. Whether you are thinking of sexual intimacy or full intercourse, it is not wise to base your decision on feelings alone.

Deciding to have sex is such an important decision that it can literally change the whole course of a person's life. If you intend to make a decision that could possibly have lifelong repercussions, you had better inform yourself about the risks. If you do not know about the long-term consequences of sexual diseases and cannot name the six most common diseases, you are crazy to think you have enough information to make a good decision. Don't be under the illusion that practising 'safe sex' will protect you from the risk of an unplanned pregnancy and the possibility of contracting sexually transmitted diseases, some of which are life-threatening.

However, there is more to making this decision than knowledge of the possible physical repercussions. No young adult is ready to have sex until they are fully educated about not just the physical consequences of the act, but the emotional and spiritual consequences that are seldom considered. Although the behaviour of peers who are sexually active might tempt you to believe that you can ignore the moral, social and religious considerations that traditionally have been considered important, the reality is that you ignore them at your peril. One cannot overestimate the power of the cultural values that exist deep within us.

What this means for you is that you are likely to develop patterns of relating as a young adult that are similar to the ways you learned to relate as a child. Imagine that you grew up in a non-tactile family, your parents were not getting along, and love, nurturing and intimacy were in short supply. It is likely that you would have learned to view affectionate male–female relationships with mistrust and suspicion and you would now find it hard to believe a person can enjoy loving, physically affectionate relationships without their leading on to full sex.

Few of us get a helpful education in school on what is normal in intimate friendships. If you are unwilling to allow yourself to be open and vulnerable, it is probable that your early experiences in your family have taught you to protect yourself from intimacy. Many young adults do not consider that a loving relationship is essential before having sex. In a strange way, it often seems easier to be sexually intimate with someone you don't know very well, someone who knows nothing of your background or family situation.

EMOTIONAL READINESS

The concept that sexual expression is closely related to expressing love for another is psychologically sound. One good way to check if you are emotionally ready for a loving sexual relationship is to look to the number of close friendships you have enjoyed. If you feel that nowhere and no one feels safe enough for you to let down your defences, you are not even close to being ready to enjoy loving sex. If you have not yet had the experience of feeling totally accepted, so that it is safe to be yourself, you have yet to have the experience of being able to trust another person fully. If you need the emotional defences that you learned to use as a young teenager to protect you from intimacy, you are setting yourself and your partner up to get hurt in your current relationship.

Good communication is a necessary prerequisite for good sex, and scores of couples who have been together for years don't have it. If you don't have the freedom to be yourself, you will never feel totally accepted. If you never talk about sex, you won't be able to ask your partner to pleasure you as you would like. If you cannot speak openly and directly about your needs, you lack trust and are probably not aware that your emotional defences are up. It is likely that you are unaware of unconsciously protecting yourself from being open, vulnerable and intimate with another person.

It is easy to make the mistake of feeling you are ready

to have sex if you believe you are old enough to be sexually responsible and plan to practise 'safe sex'. I don't want to scare you, but I must tell you that there is no contraceptive that is 100 per cent safe. Accidents are common, and although the chances of a pregnancy happening for people who practise 'safe sex' are low, failure of contraception is not as rare as you might think. Many teenage pregnancies occur because couples don't know how to meet their affectionate needs in non-sexual ways.

SEXUAL MISEDUCATION

The problem is that most people are sexually miseducated and have been led to believe that sexual desire is a sign of a need for genital sex. They are rarely taught that there is a difference between affective sex, which means meeting your intimacy needs, and genital sex, which means intercourse. They are seldom educated to understand the very basic information that sexual desire is experienced differently by men and women. Sexual desire can be a pointer that focuses your attention to other intimacy needs you may be ignoring.

Many young people feel they are ready to have sex, when their real need is to pay attention to unmet emotional needs. Until you can distinguish between lust and a need for intimacy, you are probably not even ready to think seriously about a romantic relationship. Adolescent girls tend to see love, romance and sex as being closely interlinked. Love and sex are often synonymous for women. There are some men who have no difficulty in separating sex from love.

The pace of social change in society has accelerated

so much that sexual liberation is taken for granted by modern singles. Hardly anyone believes any longer that there are good reasons to save sex for marriage. If you are in your late teens or early twenties, you will probably be muttering to yourself, 'Give me a break. I have no intention of waiting until I am married to have sex.'

Not all couples have sex in order to meet their intimacy needs and share their love. When sex is misused, it does not bring a sense of closeness or fulfilment. Some men and women are simply out to have a good time and they do not have any need for love or commitment before they make for the bedroom. They have sex rather than make love and afterwards they question if that is all there is to it.

Young men who selfishly use a woman to enjoy sexual thrills often find the experience is a disappointment – a twenty-second physiological release is seldom earth-shattering. The ecstasy that connects a couple and brings that sense of unity that makes sex so fulfilling and joyful can only be experienced when there is commitment and love.

DEFLECTING SEXUAL PRESSURE

Sexual pressure is a fact of modern life for people of all ages. Every year, many students become pregnant. Some of them are in committed relationships. Others have to deal with the consquences of a one-night stand. Many pregnancies occur when contraceptive precautions fail. This is particularly likely to happen when alcohol is involved and judgement is clouded. After a few drinks, it is easy to have sex with a partner with whom you would never consider an intimate sexual relationship if you were thinking rationally.

It's hardly surprising that so many young men and women need guidance to understand when they are ready to have sex. As soon as hormonal activity begins at puberty, young people experience sexual attraction. They fall in and out of love with amazing frequency. This falling in love has more to do with hormonal activity than it has to do with a genuine love. It can begin as early as ten or eleven years of age for girls, and a year or two later for boys, who reach puberty later.

Many adolescents are very honest about their belief that it is OK to have sex if you are in love, provided you 'feel ready' and are sexually responsible. Influenced by the advertisements for AIDS prevention, they feel it is responsible to practise 'safe sex'. There is no doubt that a significant number of young people are having sex and taking precautions against pregnancy and sexually transmitted diseases. Statistics for teenage pregnancies refer only to those who have either failed to use contraception or those whose efforts at fertility control have failed.

Unless you understand how you feel, you are unlikely to have the freedom to say exactly what you do and don't want to do with a partner. If you are not confident that you have that freedom, you are in danger of being manipulated. It is easy to be sexually coerced if you do not feel that you have the right to refuse to continue with sexual intimacy, regardless of how aroused your partner might be.

Whether we like to admit it or not, young people in the western world are made sexually vulnerable by the refusal of parents and teachers to cope with relationships and sex education in a mature and responsible way. Generations of adolescents have been damaged by repressive teaching that failed to acknowledge how important good sex is in relationships. Most of us come from families that discourage us from speaking openly about what we feel or want. One result of this is that some people feel they have no right to ask for what they want, even in marriage. Others feel that they don't have the right to refuse sexual advances, especially if they have been intimate with one another and the partner is very aroused.

It is incredible that some adults are opposed to sex education. They suggest it promotes recreational sex and encourages promiscuity. They go so far as to deny that young people are damaged when they are peer-educated and fail to receive the education that helps them to be sexually assertive and skilled in dealing with pressure. Trust me. Until you feel you can resist sexual pressure and feel confident that you can recognise manipulation and sexual deception, your decision about when to have sex will not be freely made. You are not mature enough to make good decisions about your sexual behaviour until you have the freedom to be honest about what you do and don't want to do.

Before you have sex, I believe that you should be in a committed, loving relationship. You need to have the freedom to discuss issues like contraception and sexual history that every couple that plans to have sex need to explore. Your sexual desires will be influenced by your family values, education, religion, and the cultural values accepted in your society. What you think of as your desires may not be yours – they may be your peers' desires, or your boyfriend's, or the agony aunt's checklist in your favourite magazine.

2

LOOKING FOR ROMANCE

ANNE AND BARRY

Anne felt very romantic as she and Barry hugged under the shade of the chestnut tree. It was pleasantly dark, with just enough light from the street lamps. Barry felt foolish and clumsy, but he didn't let on to Anne. He couldn't find the clasp thing to open her bra. He had seen his sister reach behind her and do something that released it, but he couldn't find any sort of clasp. All he could find was a band of elastic. He wondered if Anne put her bra on a different way. Maybe she pulled it down over her head, or perhaps there was some kind of ribbon thing in the front that tied it on. He moved his hand up the front of her jumper and felt a very small ribbon in front, but when he pulled it gently it didn't open.

When he talked to his friends, he never heard stories of any of the guys having this kind of problem. He wondered if it was a special kind of garment worn by girls with small breasts, like Anne's. Maybe she was wearing some new kind of protective bra that was designed to keep boys away from girls' breasts. He wished she'd help him, but she offered no assistance at all.

He moved around to get at it from a better angle. Anne thought he was moving to kiss her, and as she brought her face up to his, he banged her lip. He froze as he heard her groan. 'I'm sorry,' he said, wondering if he should kiss her. It might distract her from the fumbling with her bra. As his lips met hers, he felt the metal of her orthodontic braces cut against his upper lip. Barry nearly died when he tasted blood. She'd cut him. He didn't know what to do. He forced himself to swallow so he wouldn't be bleeding all over her. Then he felt sick.

His efforts to get to her breasts had failed, so he reached between her legs. 'Don't do that,' Anne said as she pushed him away. She sounded really angry. Barry had no idea of the feeling of panic that swept over her when she felt his hand moving down. She was in the middle of her period and was too inexperienced to know how Barry would react if she told him.

He wondered if she was frigid as he felt her body stiffen. 'I'd better go home,' Anne said. They walked to her house in silence. Neither of them knew what to say. Barry was afraid to kiss her in case she tasted the blood. 'See you around,' he said to Anne when they got to her house. 'Yeah,' she said, but he got the feeling that she didn't mean it.

WHAT TURNS MEN ON?

There is hardly a female alive who has not spent hours trying to figure out what men are looking for in a relationship with them. Any woman who believes she has figured it out is incredibly naive. Sexual attraction has to do with a chemistry that cannot be explained. Studies show that a man's initial reason for choosing a woman has more to do with her physical attractiveness than her personality. One *Newsweek* survey found this to be true in thirty-seven groups of men from thirty-three societies around the world.

The belief that men find women with pouting lips, big breasts and peroxided hair irresistible is widely held. There is little doubt that busty blonde pin-ups fuel the sexual fantasies of young and older men alike, but here is what you really need to hear. When guys fall in love and are ready for an intimate relationship, you would be amazed at what excites them. They seem to find the most incredibly ordinary gestures – and even unconscious facial expressions – a turn-on. Most men are fascinated by women who are well endowed but very few are so shallow that they fail to look beyond that one physical aspect of the female figure.

Did you ever wonder where this fascination for big breasts originates? Psychologists explain that men are haunted by the memory of the time when they enjoyed a perfect union with a loving mother. The theory is there is a deep desire in them to return to that sense of loving connection. I suppose you can work out the rest. The suggestion is that the arms, breasts and warmth of a woman's body remind them of the tenderness and nourishment that baby boys enjoy in the first few months of life. They have a real need as well as a desire to snuggle in there. It is also suggested that it is not just the shape of a woman's body that attracts men. The hidden need to be nurtured also plays an important part in what men want from women. I suspect that some men would suggest that this is a lot of psychobabble and has nothing to do with how they think and act. They could be right – but dare I suggest that they are not consciously aware that this is so?

VOLUPTUOUS OR VIRGINAL – WHICH IS MORE ATTRACTIVE?

It can be a comfort to slim women to discover that many men do not find curvaceous females at all enticing. Petite women make some men feel strong and protective. Others favour the less voluptuous, cool, virginal type. Others still are more attracted to brown-eyed brunettes, hazel-eyed redheads, or blue-eyed blondes. The idea that dark-haired, sallow-skinned women are more passionate than their blonde sisters is another of those myths that are still perpetuated.

There are significant differences in what males find attractive in females. The young woman wearing a slit skirt that reveals a high-laced black Doc Martin boot could be a turn-off for one guy while the image sets the heart of another pounding. A woman with pierced nipples might be a sensual delight for a teenage boy, while a slightly older man could feel pained at what he might see as body mutilation.

Sometimes young women think they are acting seductively, but they are being about as subtle as a sledgehammer. You would be surprised at how many men admit that they find the behaviour of women who set out to be sexually provocative both embarrassing and intimidating. While it is true that some men find women who take the sexual initiative a real turn-on, it is equally true that it scares others. Despite the myths to the contrary, it is not true that all men find women with bedroom eyes that promise experience in the boudoir, or anywhere else for that matter, fascinating. Even teenage boys with erupting hormones admit to being turned off by girls who are blatantly sexual and are obviously trying hard to turn them on.

This is understandable. For some men, the thrill of chasing a woman is nearly as important as catching her. When a girl makes it too easy, the challenge is removed – the excitement of the chase is gone. When a woman is there for the taking, men don't feel challenged. Guys who are prepared to use women as a sex object might avail of whatever is on offer, while other men simply lose interest.

WOMEN WHO TAKE THE INITIATIVE

Sexual attraction for both sexes is powerfully influenced by the way men and women think. Simmering hormones can be stimulated by just about anything. A girl may unconsciously reveal the nape of her neck as she pins her hair up. A guy watching her might think this is so sexy. He might find the exposure of her bare neck incredibly alluring and far more sensuous than, say, a revealing cleavage. Men can find everything a woman does sexy. The way she looks, how she moves and holds her body, her mannerisms when she speaks, the unconscious gestures she makes, her accent and even how she does her hair are all potential passion-raisers.

It is not widely recognised that the little gestures a female makes unconsciously can seem even more erotic to a male than sexy suspenders and stockings. Again, there are personal preferences involved, but some men find that when a woman goes out of her way to flaunt her body, they turn cold. Perhaps this is because too easy a target does not give that rush of adrenaline that stimulates the male hunter instincts.

When a woman puts too much effort into trying to look sexy, she may unconsciously be sending out signals that are not intended. The intention of many young women who dress to attract male interest is, 'You can look but you cannot touch'. Quite often, men misread these signals as an invitation to make advances. It is understandable that guys who have expectations of being with what they think are raunchy women are upset when their advances are rebuffed.

Sexual Harrassment

Men who assume that a sexily dressed woman must be looking for a man are under an illusion that needs to be shattered. It highlights a sexist view of women that does not stand up to examination. It also leaves men who are under this illusion exposed to the accusation of sexually harassing women. When a fellow asks a girl out, he wants to feel attractive to her. When she accepts his invitation, she affirms his male identity. In many situations, sexually miseducated men misread what is intended to be a friendly message from a female companion and imbue it with sexual connotations. I have great sympathy for the unfortunate man who upset a woman because he misread what was going on. With the most honourable of intentions, the man is bound to get it wrong if he is acting on wrong information.

Behaviour that a group of men may think of as harmless fun – ogling a woman's body, leering, standing too close or brushing up against her, making funny sexist remarks about clothing, body or sexual orientation – is experienced by most women as unpleasant sexual attention. When a woman reacts negatively, the man is often hurt and his self-esteem is damaged. Men pay a heavy price for living in a society that cannot deal with sexual matters in a healthy, factual way.

Some women who accuse men of harassing them are blamed for overreacting. There is no denying that people are confused over what constitutes genuine sexual harassment. According to the dictionary, the word 'harass' means to 'vex by repeated attacks', 'trouble', 'worry'. It ranges from sexual innuendoes, often made in the guise of teasing and fun, to coercive sexual intimacy.

Male-oriented videos and magazines are responsible for a lot of the wrong information about relationships that men believe. They fool their users into believing that fictional heroines are as readily aroused as men; virile men enjoy rough sex 'and give it to a woman hot and hard'; passionate horny women are submissive and make no demands on a partner for any kind of commitment. These are male fantasies that ignore the biological realities. Couples will not enjoy a satisfying sexual experience if they ignore their human needs. Unfortunately, poor sex education has left generations of adolescents ignorant of the differences between male and female sexual responsiveness. Some retain that ignorance in adulthood and make lousy lovers.

Men are aroused instantaneously and cool down just as quickly after an orgasm that lasts seconds. Women are slower to get turned on and when they are, they probably enjoy sex more than men, having much longer orgasms. A woman has the only organ in the human body that is made specifically to give pleasure – her clitoris. Couples who are ignorant of these facts do not understand how to enjoy great sex.

THE ALL-CONQUERING MALE HERO MYTH

The myth of the all-conquering male hero who is irresistible and has women falling at his feet needs to be scotched. There is no harm in men daydreaming, but any man who believes these myths is living in cloud-cuckoo-land. Sexual equality has changed the attitude of women. Any intelligent guy who looks around him can see that these portrayals of the fair sex bear little resemblance to the vast majority of the women he knows. Some women might even find the term 'fair sex' condescending and offensive. Yet it is astonishing to find some men who still hold on to those illusions because they simply don't have more reliable or accurate information with which to replace them.

Young men who base their relationship needs and sexual wants on these stereotypical images have learned the wrong lessons about sex. If such beliefs are not challenged, unfortunate young males will continue to make unwanted sexual advances to females in the mistaken belief that this is what they expect. When a woman refuses the advances of a man, he is bound to feel rejected and hurt. If his self-esteem is damaged, he may even blame the women for being a tease.

Understanding Sexual Pressure

The majority of young people get their sex education from dubious sources. Generations of adolescents have been educated about sex by their friends behind bicycle sheds and in locker rooms. Peer-education is usually value-free. It encourages performance anxiety, dangerous attitudes to promiscuity, casual and unsafe sex and condones sex that treats women as sexual objects.

Sexually miseducated people get a lot of information from song lyrics, videos and magazines. One only has to watch music videos to see how viewers are bombarded by constant sexual imagery, promoting unrealistic expectations of sex that are unhelpful and unhealthy. Both sexes are vulnerable to getting hurt when they are given false expectations of sexual intimacy based on illusion and sexual fantasy. It's a real eye-opener to see how sexy bed-scenes in films are shot. The illusions are brilliant. On the screen it looks hot. Behind the scenes, the girl is acting to the camera and the guy she is supposed to be with may not even be in the bed with her. What I find so sad about all of this is that so many young people actually believe that exciting sex should mirror what they see on the screen. That mistaken belief kills their own natural spontaneity. It gives them a false concept against which to measure themselves, usually to their own detriment.

The belief that young men should be out trying to get laid puts a pressure on young males. It is socially acceptable for men to brag to each other about their sexual conquests. This boasting is not as harmless as it may at first appear. It creates hidden pressures that encourage young guys to go out and achieve sexual conquests so that they too can look manly. It breeds performance anxiety in men and fosters the mindset that you can tell women you love them and, after sex, leave them.

Young people who are having sex are seldom aware that they are not making free choices. They don't understand that they are coerced into sexual activity by pressures that they do not consciously recognise. The sexual pressure on adolescents, generated by the expectations of their peers, is very powerful and often encourages young people to have under-age sex. The need to appear macho forces many young men into premature sexual activity, before they are emotionally ready for such encounters. Physically, they may enjoy the sex, but quite often that enjoyment is also tinged with guilty feelings and worries. A man can be charged with statutory rape and jailed for having sex with a girl who is under age.

When a young man believes it is unmanly to miss a sexual opportunity, he feels obliged to make sexual advances to women. At one level, he may not even want to have sex. He may feel bad about putting pressure on a woman to see how far he can go. Even if he is successful with his conquests, he may end up harbouring doubts about using women that make him feel unsure and can have a devastating effect on how he feels about himself as a person.

THE MALE STUD OR GIGOLO

Although men are brought up on the idea of the male who is out to get sex wherever he can find it, few aspire to being labelled the local stud. Men have ambivalent feelings about the portrayal of the stud who has selfish disregard for women's feelings, health or pregnancy. The vast majority of men are sexually responsible and do not set out to use women selfishly. This does not mean that they are sensitive lovers. It just means that they try their best within the limitations of the information they have. As Maya Angelou says, 'when they know better, they do better'.

When you realise how much wrong and inaccurate information people have, it becomes easier to understand why men cannot clearly say what they want from women in a relationship. Few men are sufficiently in touch with their feelings to be able to communicate honestly about their sexual or emotional needs. They are not to blame for this. It is the fault of a society that fails to teach men and women about the differences in the needs that men and women have for sex and intimate communication.

Emotional Intimacy

The belief that a man who wants an intimate relationship with a woman can only achieve this through sex is widespread. It is simply not true. Intimacy does not necessarily entail sexual intimacy. Sexual intimacy does not confer the ability to communicate intimately. While it is true that men feel safe in expressing love and intimacy through sex, it is certainly not the only way to meet these needs. Unfortunately, many men simply don't understand this or know how to satisfy their emotional needs outside a sexual relationship.

A man may have ambivalent feelings about intimacy. One part of him wants to express love and feel intimate. However, those feelings make him vulnerable. Most men are divided between the desire to be nurtured and minded and the fear that accepting tenderness and intimacy is an unmanly thing to do. If men could talk to each other about personal feelings and what they are experiencing in their relationships the way most women do, they could get the reassurance they so badly want.

For far too long, the advertisers' dream couple was a dominant man and a compliant woman. These stereotypes may fulfil romantic fantasies but this unequal combination is not a good model for honest communication between men and women. Our society tells boys that men need to be dominant, competitive, powerful and masterful. Masters and Johnson, the world-renowned sex therapists, say, 'We live in a society that trains and encourages females to be victims of sexual coercion and males to victimise females.'

We cannot not communicate. Our voices, eyes and bodies are always sending out messages. How they are interpreted is deeply influenced by the assumptions others make. Many men are equally poor at interpreting and at communicating their needs and wants. One reason for this is that they are out of touch with their feelings and cannot find the words to say what it is they want. To have a satisfying relationship, it is important for both partners to be open about their wants, needs and dreams.

Many men cherish the belief that their girlfriend, partner or spouse is a mind-reader and will instinctively know how to take care of all his emotional needs. If a man is not consciously aware of his own desires and is not able to talk honestly about his needs, he is probably unaware that he has exaggerated expectations of the relationship.

Much of what happens between men and women is coloured by such unrealistic romantic expectations. The idyllic dreams of many young couples remain unfulfilled because they have little connection with mundane, real life.

During the early stages of a loving relationship, many women put pressure on men to make a commitment. When virginity was prized, men accused women of using sex to trap them into getting married. Most men fail to realise that sex is often so intimately connected with love for a woman that she cannot separate them. Some men separate love and sex quite easily. This is why you find married men who have been accused of having an affair telling their wives, 'She didn't mean anything to me. It is you that I truly love.'

ATTITUDES AND EXPECTATIONS

Social scientists tell us that the great importance society attaches to romantic love is partly to blame for the huge increase in the break-up of relationships. It is sad but true that the less experienced a guy is sexually, the more unlikely he is to realise that his perceptions of what women want are inaccurate. Most young men find it hard to believe that genuine sex appeal must go beyond the physical – a woman's appearance, body shape or breast size – and relate to the whole person.

What men want from women is strongly influenced by self-esteem; the attitude to, and expectations of women he has picked up from his family; the attitudes of his peers to relationships and commitment; the expectations of his culture and society. Since it is not good for a man's self-esteem to admit that he is ignorant and needs to be educated about how to relate to a woman, particularly about how to relate sexually, he is seldom free to ask for the information he needs. One result of this male ignorance is the enormous performance pressure men put on themselves. The idea that virile men are always ready, willing and able to have sex focuses on the physical and shows little understanding of satisfying the emotional or spiritual needs that are so important in feeling good about oneself.

PARENTAL INFLUENCES

Most men are unaware of how influenced their concept of sexy women is by their parents' values and standards. What many of us think of as *our* feelings are often based more on the standards and attitudes of our parents than on our own instincts. Numerous people influence how we think and feel about our relationships. Brothers and sisters, grandparents, friends, teachers, television programmes, even famous people we have never met teach us to have expectations about what is desirable and socially acceptable in relationships.

The assumption that as teenage boys mature physically and emotionally they will naturally develop healthy relationship skills does not stand up to examination. Parents are the primary educators of children. They provide the role models on which adolescents base their expectations of adult relationships. If a boy's father treated his mother like a queen he will probably go on to treat women with great courtesy and respect. If he saw his parents treat each other in a disrespectful way, his adult behaviour will probably mirror what he saw in the home.

Peer Influences

We have already seen how peer-educated lads are ignorant about the importance of foreplay and fail to understand that women have different sexual needs to men. So many young men do what they think is expected of the macho male, and are unaware that the experience is neither pleasurable nor exciting for their partner. It is not widely admitted that adolescent sex is frequently a rather disappointing experience. It's a twenty-second wonder for the man. When he discovers that his partner is not certain whether penetration occurred, his ego is dented. He may feel selfish. His perceived failure as a caring lover is damaging to his self-image, the relationship and particularly to his girlfriend, who may feel she was used by him for his selfish pleasure.

Too many young adults who have sex end up angry, feeling frustrated and used, when sex does not measure up to their expectations. This is particularly true of inexperienced young people who have bought into the popular myth that the earth should move, and when they find it doesn't, they are left wondering who is at fault. 'Is there something wrong with me or with her?'

Stereotypes Accepted By Society

There is no denying that adolescent boys have a powerful sex drive. Some have no reservations about setting out to use women sexually without any care for their feelings. Influenced by the stereotype of the man who wants to enjoy sexual intimacy without engaging emotionally, they do not understand that they are hurting both themselves and their partner.

Female stereotypes are reinforced for young men by a small number of women who feel that they have to fulfil male sexual fantasies to be attractive. When a woman makes the needs of a man more important than her own needs, it is often a signal that there will be trouble ahead. In the beginning, she will be happy to agree with his wishes. After a while, she will begin to feel resentful that they always end up doing what he wants. Then comes the stage where she is telling herself, 'If he really loved me, he would be more sensitive to my needs and treat me better.'

She pays a heavy price for not listening to her own needs and talking honestly about what she wants. If a woman's emotional needs are not being met, this will be mirrored in her sexual relationship. She probably won't enjoy the sex. In a relationship where two inadequate people are using each other sexually, there is seldom honest communication. Adolescent boys who are sexually miseducated are at a huge disadvantage in their relationships with the opposite sex.

Many a young man who wants to have an intimate relationship with a girl fails to understand how important talking is for women. It creates a sense of closeness. It is almost as if some women need to bare their thoughts and feel listened to before they have the security to bare their breasts. Communication is the secret of all warm, loving relationships. When partners have the freedom to be open and honest with each other, they are well on the road to enjoying the emotional intimacy that in time can lead to a deeply loving relationship, where both people are comfortable and have no need to play roles.

Avoiding Intimacy

It is not uncommon for women to accuse men of craving sex and withholding love. I suspect that one reason for this is the emotional detachment that is encouraged in boys in their early years. Young males are trained to be strong, independent, competitive and in control. If they reveal their tender feelings, they are likely to be labelled a 'wimp'. The only emotion they are not encouraged to repress is anger. As a result of this emotional detachment, boys learn to avoid intimacy.

By avoiding intimacy, men miss out on a whole range of emotional experiences that are crucial to understanding how to get what they want in a relationship with women. Men who crave sex and withhold love are often seeking intimacy in the only way they know. Sex for them is not as integral a part of love as it is for some women, for whom sex and love are seen as the same thing. While it is true that the behaviour of some men is selfish and uncaring, this is an accusation that it is unfair to level at men as a group. I do not believe that the majority of men want to use women only for their own satisfaction.

When it comes to the vitally important question of serious sex appeal, what most men want from a women is not the fantasy perfection of a sexy figure, but a partner who will make them feel loved and accepted for who they are. Unfortunately, this does not happen as easily as it used to, even in the very recent past. Girls are no longer eager to settle down, marry the man of their dreams and have his babies. Educational opportunities for girls have radically altered their expectations of careers and family life. Young women nowadays decline to make a commitment in relationships until they have established a career for themselves. Few aspire to staying at home to look after a husband or children. Some view marriage so negatively that it is now becoming as difficult for young men to find a wife or life partner as it has always been for older women to find husbands.

The rapid rise in cohabitation is indicative of the changing mores in society. Increasingly, it looks as if living together is replacing the more traditional engagement. Twenty-five years ago, only 6 per cent of brides in Britain lived with their prospective husband before marriage. This figure has now risen to 60 per cent. The modern couple tend to cohabit for about five years. They then either marry or end the relationship. Those who marry are over four times more likely to split up than couples who get married without living together first. As women become choosier about what they want from a relationship, men are finding it more difficult to meet a suitable mate and hold on to her.

3

Early Sexual Pressure

'Girls only want lads who have a huge six-pack and bulging biceps,' said John, who was acting as spokesperson for his buzz group. It was a mixed class and the teacher had separated the students into single-sex groups to discuss what boys and girls are looking for in friendships. The question for discussion was open-ended, as the students were very young. Yet, in that class of 30 students, each group of 13- and 14-year-olds decided to focus on relationships with the other sex. Every group had elected a spokesperson to report back at the end of their discussion. John's friends nodded their agreement as he spoke. Before he could continue, one of the girls jumped to her feet and – in a very aggressive way – took over.

John stood sheepishly as Sarah retorted angrily, 'No they don't.' She was strongly dismissive of what the boys said. 'It's not true that girls only look for appearance. We think that it's the personality that counts. Some girls just want love, but guys are too immature to understand. Everything they say is sexually orientated. Guys think of sex twenty-four hours a day.'

VULNERABLE BABES

John and Sarah are both fourteen years of age, and it is very clear from their interaction that they and their friends are sexually aware. In western society, children are being initiated into sexual behaviour – intimate kissing, cuddling and mutual masturbation – at an earlier age than ever before. Researchers have documented the sequence of how intimate behaviour progresses. They estimate that it now takes about two years for adolescents to move from necking to intimate touching and finally to intercourse. The tragedy is that with all of this information in the public forum, so little is done to help boys and girls to enjoy their middle childhood without having to deal with the peer pressure that pushes many into premature sexually intimate behaviour.

Many older teenagers and young adults don't cope particularly well with sexual pressure. Usually it's because they feel so uncomfortable in the situation that they are not thinking clearly. Whenever there is media publicity about a twelve-year-old who is pregnant, we hear concerned parents interviewed. Everybody agrees that youngsters are being asked to cope with sexual pressures that are way beyond their ability to handle. It's usually clear that these parents are aware that many youngsters don't even have a sufficient grasp of the basic facts of life to begin to understand how peer pressure influences their behaviour.

In an ideal world, vulnerable children would be taught to understand that they are harmed when they allow peer pressure to control their behaviour. Parents would act responsibly and make sure that children were not pressured sexually or exploited by their peers. They would give them every opportunity to discuss how to deal with powerful sexual feelings and desires, to understand that although they are physically capable of becoming parents and have the normal desires that are created by active hormones, emotionally they are not ready to deal with those feelings, or with pregnancy.

We don't live in an ideal world. In reality, most parents simply don't feel comfortable, and say they do not have the confidence to undertake this task. Teachers who deal with the topic in schools are not much more successful, because schools are so concerned with protecting the innocence of children that they fail to give timely information. The time to encourage boys and girls to delay getting involved in sexual activity is before they start. This could be as early as eight or nine years of age for some girls. Once they become romantically involved, it is already too late. Many adult men and women who felt hurt and rejected by how a young partner treated them in their early teens carry the scars of their bad experiences from adolescence into adulthood.

SEX EDUCATION – TOO LITTLE, TOO LATE

There is a widespread belief that better sex education could do a lot to lower the number of teenage pregnancies and minimise the emotional damage done to children who are sexually exploited by immature peers. There isn't a great deal of evidence to support the view that school programmes are effective. I believe this is because the consumers – the students in schools – are rarely consulted or invited to evaluate these programmes. The feedback from the small number of students who are asked their opinion is that sex education is too little, too late.

Young people lack information at the time they need it most. How can they be expected to make informed decisions about their sexual behaviour when they depend on magazines and their peers for information, information that is not always to be trusted? It's too late to wait until the middle teenage years to tackle the thorny subject of teenage pregnancy. For some twelve-year-old students, sex is already a topic of discussion. The peer pressure is on – strongly. Young boys are under pressure to measure up to the expectations some females have of how the male body should look. These are based on the athletic physiques of film stars and bodybuilders.

Boys and men seem to be well able to sense when girls and women are unhappy and dissatisfied with them. However, males are not so good at working out what exactly the problem is. The communication between fourteen-year-old John and Sarah mirrors the communication of twenty-year-olds, forty-year-olds and seventy-year-olds. Let's break it down and observe a very common pattern of communication, where no one is really listening.

John thought he knew what Sarah's group wanted because he knew that girls were unhappy with how boys looked. He tried to tell her what boys thought. She didn't acknowledge what he said at all. Instead, she jumped right in with both guns blazing, and spelled out how boys have got it all wrong. This was a harsh put-down for them. Neither had any sensitivity to the fact that men and women communicate in different ways. Until all young people learn to understand about assertive communication and are taught to be sensitive to the differences there are in male and female communication, they are bound to experience problems.

It's illogical to think that young adolescents like John and Sarah can deal with sexual pressure if they are not taught how to do so. The nub of the problem is that parents are the primary teachers of children, and if they don't have effective communication skills, it will be impossible for their children to have them either. Children learn from watching how their parents relate, and if we are really honest, we have to acknowledge that the majority of parents probably have lots of room for improvement in the way they talk and listen to each other.

Anyone who works with couples who have relationships difficulties will hear the complaint, 'He never talks to me.' The woman involved believes this and, from her perspective, she is correct. A far more accurate assessment would be that the couple simply do not know how to listen to each other. One result of a failure to listen is that talking makes the gap between them wider, rather than bringing them closer together.

The truth is that both sexes are very poor at communicating what they need from each other. People are fully convinced that they have asked for what they want, but they rarely check out what the other person understands by their request. Let's go back to John and Sarah. Don't assume that because they are only teenagers, you have nothing to learn from their situation. The same communication skills that they need are effective at every stage of life.

ASSUMPTIONS

When you are learning to communicate, it is vital to understand that the way you think and the assumptions you make about how another person thinks may be accurate or may be totally inaccurate. Most of us assume that our family and friends feel exactly the same way that we do, when in fact they may have very different feelings and attitudes.

Communication involves three things: talking, listening and thinking. It's said that God gave us two ears and only one mouth because we are meant to listen twice as much as we speak. Listening involves hearing the words, and this is important. However, much more important than listening to the words is listening for the feelings – what I call 'heart listening'. Sadly, many highly educated and competent adults have never learned to listen for more than the words. They have never been taught that the words are only 7 per cent of communication: they miss out on the feelings and fail to connect at a heart level. This is where real contact is made and closeness and intimacy are experienced.

The brief exchange between John and Sarah would have made a totally different impact on everyone concerned if they had had better listening skills. Just suppose that Sarah had shown that she heard what bothered the boys *before* she told them what the girls felt was wrong. Would it have made a difference? Let's suppose they had a lesson on assertive communication and they learned how to really listen. The scenario might have gone like this:

'Girls want only lads who have a huge six-pack and

bulging biceps,' said John, who was acting as spokesperson for his buzz group. John's friends nodded their agreement as he spoke. Before he could continue, one of the girls jumped to her feet and, in what appeared to be a very aggressive way, said, 'It sounds as if you think girls want only lads who have a huge six-pack and bulging biceps. No, they don't.' Immediately, the boys felt validated because Sarah mirrored back that she heard what they said. The tension evaporates from a confrontation when people feel heard. Can you see how Sarah's use of reflective listening made it more likely that the boys would pay attention? If they had been taught that they too were expected to be able to put what she says to them in their own words, and confirm that they have heard her correctly, they would be less likely to switch off. Many people don't listen well enough to be able to reflect back what they are hearing. They are too busy deciding on what to say in reply.

In a learning situation, it would be suggested that Sarah could now check if she is picking up how the boys are feeling. She might say something like, 'You sound angry, as if you think that it's unfair.' You may think that is rather a lot to expect, but many young adolescents can put adults to shame because they pick up these skills so quickly. For older people, learning to sense how others feel is a necessary part of good communication.

In theory, if Sarah said, 'It's not true that girls only look for appearance. We think that it's the personality that counts. Some girls just want love, but guys are too immature to understand. Everything they say is sexually orientated. Guys think of sex twenty-four hours a day', there is a much better chance of having the kind of discussion that will lead to a resolution that makes each sex more aware of what the other wants from them. In practice, the girls are probably correct about the boys' lack of maturity, and it is highly unlikely that they would remember all the girls' points, or allow themselves to be vulnerable in a big group.

Pressure on Minors

Isn't it sad that very young children pick up the concept that friendships between boys and girls point towards relationships that involve pressure to be sexually intimate? It's simply not good enough for adults to opt out and say they want to keep children innocent. They can't. Their efforts only keep children ignorant. We live in a highly sexualised society and the effect of this aspiration to keep children innocent is the denial of the education about relationships that they so desperately need. There is a wise old saying, 'Where there's a will, there's a way.' If the will is there to do something to make middle-childhood less sexually pressured, then the money and the spin doctors will be found to show how it can be done.

Girls are always rather proud that they grow up and develop physically earlier than boys. They need to know that coming on to a boy who is smaller physically, even thought he may be the same age, is probably unfair. He is unlikely to have reached puberty yet, and may very well be too young to have that special interest in girls. Boys need to feel as comfortable with a girl when they are with a group of their friends as they do when they are with her on their own. If they don't, they are not ready for a relationship that involves romance.

Satisfying relationships always involve good communication. If a man or woman, regardless of their age, cannot say 'no' to something they dislike or don't want to do without feeling under pressure from a partner, they need to step back and recognise that they lack freedom in the relationship. One person is trying to control the other. Many young adults do not have the communication skills to decline an invitation without sounding as if they are rejecting the other person. They allow themselves to be manipulated into doing things they don't want to do because they feel vulnerable and lack the confidence to be honest.

CHILDREN NEED THE WHOLE PICTURE

Some parents and teachers believe that you cannot stop young people having sex. They believe that the best that can be done is to make sure that youngsters are well versed about the importance of contraceptive protection. This is a not a solution, because it is dealing only with part of the problem. It fails to give the full story that young people need if they are to make informed decisions. It doesn't even deal very comprehensively with the physical risks, and ignores the emotional and spiritual aspects that are equally important to the rounded development of the whole person.

The AIDS prevention advertisements that say, 'safe sex: wear a condom' get that message across well. They make it clear that condoms offer protection against unwanted pregnancy and infection with the human immunodeficiency virus (HIV). What they fail to advertise with the same strong impact is that the protection extends only to the part of the body that is covered by the sheath and there are other nasty viral infections that can be passed on through sexual contact to the areas of the genitals that are not covered. Turn to Chapter 9 for more information on sexually transmitted diseases. The belief that boys and girls do not need this information until they are legally old enough to have sex needs to be challenged. If a person is with a partner who has a sexually transmitted disease (STD) that is caused by a virus, he or she is at risk of contracting that disease.

It's Hard to Tell Love from Lust at Any Age
Teenagers who have little information about powerful sexual feelings are not in a position to discover whether they are in love or in lust. Many adults face exactly the same dilemma, because the two feelings are frequently experienced in very similar ways. It would be foolish to think that age makes it easier to deal with strong sexual desires. The hormones may be a bit less active, but they still simmer away, and in some situations, lust acts like the weight on a pressure cooker which causes a head of steam to build up inside. Feelings that are ignored or denied or not given attention do not go away; they simmer on. Feelings that are acknowledged are not as dangerous. Once they are recognised, it takes the pressure away and makes it easier to deal with them.

It's difficult for most people, whether single or married, to have the freedom to be assertive and speak openly about what they want to do and don't want to do sexually. It's next to impossible for adolescents, who believe it is cool to act in grown-up ways and who lack maturity to be sexually assertive. Many lack basic biological information about reproduction, and some, who are influenced by the pornographic videos they have watched, don't even know what normal people do when they have sex.

Many, many people simply don't have the vocabulary, social skills or assertiveness to deal well with demanding partners. We all know that adolescents are like babes in the wood: extremely vulnerable to being exploited. We are not so open about all the adult relationships where people in positions of trust and authority misuse their power and exploit others for their own selfish ends. In the recent past, it was assumed, wrongly, that this was the preserve of men. It's not, and more and more cases are being brought against women who have sexually harassed their male staff.

It's so easy for an impressionable youngster to think that they are being shown love, when in reality they are being sexually exploited. There is no denying that a number of immature, under-age children believe they are in love and agree to engage in consensual sex. Some, like the unfortunate thirteen-year-old Sarah Louise in the television soap *Coronation Street* had sex just once and found herself pregnant. I'm not condoning sex between minors when I say that it's understandable. It's a clear indication that they are using sex to meet emotional needs.

Many young people meet their needs for closeness and affection through sex. It is important to understand that although the majority of pre-teenage children are curious about what sex feels like – who does what and how that feels – and have strong sexual urges, the majority try not to act on those feelings. Studies show that the children who enjoy good communication with their parents, especially with their mother, are more likely to delay sexual activity. When they do have sex, they are also more likely to act responsibly and use protection.

Those who do not have their needs for affection met at home are more likely to use sex to meet their needs. Once hormonal activity begins, sexual desires begin to emerge. Parents are seldom ready to accept the idea of pre-teenage children dealing with sexual feelings and desires. Like the ostrich who sticks his head in the sand, they refuse to open their eyes and acknowledge the facts that are there for all to see. Children are sexual people.

Children Are Sexual People

Children are reaching puberty earlier. We don't know why this is. It could be caused by better nutrition or because of hormones in food. Whatever the reasons, the fact remains. Young boys and girls experience feelings of sexual attraction, wet dreams and periods years before their parents had to deal with these matters when they were growing up. No one in their right mind would suggest that it is acceptable for such young children to satisfy their sexual curiosity through sexual intimacy with the opposite sex. Yet the reality is that some do.

Under-age Sex

Whether we like to admit it or not, there is a great deal of sexual activity among adolescents. Only a tiny number of teenagers who are sexually active have intercourse and go on to have babies. Many who engage in mutual masturbation and oral sex believe they are simply fooling around, and deny that this is 'engaging in sexual activity'. It's frightening to find how widespread the belief is among young people that if you are in love and you use protection to avoid pregnancy and sexually transmitted diseases then it's OK to have sex. Although they are usually aware of the legal age for sex, in most countries they ignore it with impunity. They have very logical reasons for doing so, because they rarely know of anyone who has had to deal with the legal consequences. The belief that the police are not interested in prosecuting minors who engage in under-age sex is well-founded. Many sexually active teenagers have friends or family members who were a party to a teenage pregnancy and they weren't charged. One result of this is that it is becoming more difficult for the young people who want to argue that they are below the legal age, to use this as an excuse not to have sex.

Young boys have always masturbated, and the modern young girl, who is influenced by what she reads in teenage magazines, is likely to try to get to know how her own body works. She masturbates too, and often the underlying reason is so that she can find out what satisfies her sexually, and tell her boyfriend how to stimulate her. Effective relationship education, whether at home or in school, involves listening to children and what they believe about normal adolescent behaviour. Forbidding them to have relationships is not the answer to changing attitudes. Teaching them that in every situation they have choices, and allowing them the space to think about and discuss the consequences of the different choices they can make, is a far better way to inspire fresh thinking.

SOME CONSEQUENCES OF PREMATURE SEXUAL ACTIVITY
For the moment, let's ignore all moral and religious arguments that discourage premarital sex and just explore the consequences of premature sexual activity. The rate of teenage pregnancy is alarmingly high. In countries where abortion is available, it is estimated that about half of teen pregnancies end in termination. A large number of the men who father children desert their partner and leave the girl alone to deal with the trauma of an unplanned pregnancy. Not all men who fail to play a part in their child's life do so from choice. In many cases, the mother decides to have nothing further to do with her child's father. It is very painful for a teenage father who wants his girlfriend to have his baby to discover that he can legally do nothing to prevent her from having an abortion.

Single teenage mothers left to bring a child up on their own have a really tough time. They usually have to leave school without any qualifications, so even when they are in a position to work, they end up in poorly-paid employment. The majority of single mothers are caught in a poverty trap. They are more likely to become young grandmothers. Studies show that the adolescent children of single parents become sexually active earlier than their counterparts in two-parent families. They have less supervision when there is only one parent around. If that parent is dating, that also has an influence on behaviour. Few single parents want history repeating itself, yet it frequently does.

4

UNDERSTANDING PEER PRESSURE

SHEENA'S TALE

I remember Sheena, a fifteen-year-old girl, telling me about her experiences with Mike, her eighteen-year-old boyfriend. She believed he really cared about her. They could talk about anything and felt really close before they had sex. Afterwards, everything changed. 'It was so awful. I didn't know that sex could hurt. I thought it would be nice and we'd be really close and sexy. It was horrible, painful and hurt really badly. Afterwards, I felt terrible. I hated everything about it. I felt dirty, like he'd used me. It felt like he just wanted to relieve himself and that was it. I never wanted to see him again. He didn't care about me. He's a rotten, selfish f---er. All he wanted was sex. The worst part is that he told his pals. He boasted to his mates that he'd done it with me. I'm really worried that some of the girls in school will think that I'm a slag, or that my brother will hear about it and tell at home.'

VIRGINITY CAN BE LOST ONLY ONCE

Sheena felt she lost something important that night and it's true, she did. She lost her virginity, and she can never get it back. Before she had sex, she hadn't really put any value on virginity, probably because many of her friends had lost theirs and nobody considered that it was a big deal. She anticipated that she'd lose hers as soon as she turned sixteen, and found it hard to understand why she felt so upset.

When we talked, she came to the insight that she really couldn't judge whether she was in love or not. The truth was she felt under a lot of pressure to have sex and didn't recognise how stressed she was. She knew that boys usually want to do more than girls. With hindsight, she was able to admit to herself that Mike put her under a lot of pressure. She only agreed to 'do it' to keep him interested. She was afraid he was going to dump her if she didn't agree. She had put him off a few times, but she knew he wouldn't wait around for ever. If boys had waited for a few weeks and didn't get sex, she believed they would move on.

Like many other vulnerable teenagers, she made the mistake of thinking that if Mike could come to her for sex, he wouldn't want anyone else. Poor Sheena couldn't have been more wrong. Guys like Mike, who have a reputation for liking younger girls, usually don't stay around after they get what they wanted all along – sex.

REALITY TEST

Parents in every generation fail to recognise that you can't stop adolescents experimenting sexually. A shocking number of parents think that the majority of sixteen-year-olds who are romantically involved limit their sexual activity to a kiss and a cuddle. While this is true of about half of that age group, the other half have moved on to sexual behaviour that carries risks for the sexually ignorant. By the age of sixteen, 50 per cent of teenagers have allowed genital touching, 33 per cent have 'fingered' a partner or engaged in a 'hand job', the popular slang for mutual masturbation. The majority regret it the next day, especially when alcohol was involved.

The erroneous belief that having sex creates feelings of closeness and will make the other person fall in love is well established among the teen population, mostly among young women. It's clear that the majority are ignorant about how one is likely to feel in the cold light of the following day, when it's embarrassing to admit that yes, you were really screwed by that one. Sex alters how a woman sees her lover. Some women have never heard of oxytocin, a bonding hormone that is produced by a female during lovemaking.

One reason why people in long-term relationships become more accepting of a partner's foibles after sex is that it creates a kind of amnesia that makes them forget minor details. The little things about the partner that used to make them annoyed or irritated seem unimportant after good sex. Other women have such a ghastly experience that sex turns them right off their partner. When a young male is inexperienced and has intercourse without foreplay and none of the romantic preliminaries that are so necessary from the woman's point of view, it can be a physically painful experience for her. A girl who is madly in love with a guy and thinks he feels the same about her can be devastated after such a sexual encounter. Sadly, such experiences are surprisingly common and will continue where there is poor communication.

THE OTHER HALF DON'T

The old fashioned question, 'Are a few moments of pleasure worth a lifetime of regret?' is as relevant today as it ever was. There is no denying that teenagers have powerful sexual feelings and it is only natural to expect that they will respond to their natural instincts and experiment sexually. It is also to be expected that peer-educated young people who have a frightening amount of incorrect information will make risky decisions. Even college students and young adults are poorly informed about the risks they run by having sex too soon, or with the wrong person. A single sexual experience with a partner who carries a viral sexual infection like HIV can have fatal consequences.

Adults cannot deny that teenagers have always experimented sexually. For the vast majority, that experimentation takes place within a relationship where at least one person is in love, but not always. More and more adolescents have casual relationships because they feel they have to live up to their friends' expectations. If you believe that all your friends are doing it and you're not, you'll feel the odd one out. When you have correct and accurate, up-to-date information, it takes some of the pressure off you.

The contraceptive pill, abortion and other technological changes make it harder to refuse to have sex. As methods of avoiding and terminating pregnancy become more readily available, it becomes more difficult for teenagers to hold on to their virginity. In the past, the fear of an unwanted pregnancy gave young people a good excuse to refuse to have sex. That excuse is gone now. Many young women would expect to be laughed at if they refused to have sex because they claimed a strong belief in virginity.

While it is true that having sex is taken for granted by 50 per cent of sixteen-year-olds, it's equally true that half the teenagers in that age group don't make that assumption. This little nugget of accurate information has incredible potential to free young people from sexual pressure. We have already seen that peer pressure powerfully influences the behaviour of teenagers who have sex early. Peer pressure is perceived as coming only from friends and fellow students. Certainly, the opinions of friends are important, but the stress that is experienced from peer pressure comes from the person's own thinking.

Let me explain, because this mistaken attitude to peer pressure is so widespread that practically every teenager accepts it and hardly any parent or teacher challenges its inaccuracy. If I were to go into any class of sixteen-year-olds and suggest that from now on I wanted each person in that class to ask the person beside them to choose whether they should have sex or not, there would be an uproar, and rightly so. Students would suggest I was a crank who had no right to tell them what to do. Yet these same young people would be unlikely to have any awareness of how they allow the approval of their peers to influence the choices they make about sex. Teens fool themselves into believing that they are making a free choice, when they are not.

Let's try to understand. The idea that peer pressure comes from outside is only partly true. The really powerful pressure comes from how a person thinks. You can understand that a person who believes that all his friends are having sex is put under pressure. We both know that the friends rarely stand around insisting that a guy or girl loses their virginity. I say rarely, because it wouldn't be fair to deny that among a small number of adolescents there is intense pressure to 'have it off' or be picked on. When peers have that kind of power, and adolescents are afraid to be assertive, you can be sure that the young people in that group are immature and have unresolved self-esteem issues.

A lack of assertiveness is always rooted in fear: fear that you mightn't be liked, fear that you will be rejected, that you will be teased or thrown out of the group or that people will think you are different. When you understand that peer pressure is rooted in fear, you can begin to find ways of overcoming that fear. It often happens that when one person in a group has the courage to speak out and refuse to go along with the pressure, others chime in and back them up. All it takes is one person of courage to bring about change.

Boys probably have a more stressful time with peer pressure than girls because males frequently lie and claim they had sex when they did not. Friends who jibe at boys and tease them about 'getting nothing' and 'not doing it' put teens under enormous pressure. It's understandable that lads feel they have to be in with their friends. They have wrong information, so they worry that if everyone has done it, they are different. Anxiety about a low sex drive is all too common among boys who have boastful friends. Immature young girls are frequently exploited sexually by older boys.

IMPORTANT CULTURAL VALUES
In early adolescence, it's perfectly normal to feel you have to be like your friends when you're with them. Almost

everyone learns by looking at what their friends are doing and behaving like them in order to fit in and feel accepted. Young people cover up how insecure and embarrassed they really feel by putting on a brave face and pretending to be more confident than they are. Both sexes act with a lot of bravado so everyone appears outwardly confident, while inside they are going through the normal adolescent insecurities.

Although the behaviour of peers who are sexually active might tempt you to believe that you can disregard the moral, social and religious considerations that your parents hold dear, you really can't ignore the beliefs your family cherishes without paying a price. Regardless of how you feel about accepting or rejecting values that were traditionally considered important in your culture, the reality is that you cannot escape their influence. If your views and values mirror those of your peers, but are out of step with what is believed to be important in your family, be prepared for personal conflict that will bring you to what I call soul-searching. Dr Ellen McGrath says that one cannot overestimate the power of cultural values that exist deep within us. Our values dictate how we must behave and what roles are 'right' and 'wrong', feminine and masculine, appropriate and inappropriate.

When we go against the values our families consider important, we end up feeling guilty. If you've ever had the experience of feeling bad after you have been with someone, without really understanding why, the chances are that you have acted against the family's values, which are buried somewhere deep within you. You feel guilty because you have failed to live up to their expectations.

Soul-searching is another way to describe spirituality. It brings you to self-knowledge. Spirituality leads us to this awareness of who we are and what we feel and believe. Soul-searching for some people is tied in with organised religion, but for many others, it's not. Don't get confused by the words 'religion' and 'spirituality'. Many people wrongly assume that if you don't go to church and worship within a community of believers, you have lost your religion and are without spirituality. That's a really narrow viewpoint. You can reject the teachings of your religion but you cannot lose your spirituality.

A large number of the teenagers with whom I work have rejected religions and are spiritually adrift, with no guidance. They act like puppets, letting other people pull their strings to make them move. They don't have the freedom to think for themselves, so they go along with the crowd. They think they are making decisions about their own behaviour when they reject church teaching, and fail to see that, all the time, their friends or peer pressure control what they do. They confuse freedom and manipulation. They are controlled by the beliefs teenagers share about how they should look and what they should do. In every generation, peer-educated teens make decisions based on incorrect information and dangerous myths that are rooted in society and as difficult to eradicate as noxious weeds.

MISTAKES TEACH LIFE LESSONS

Frequently parents and other caring adults see young people who are totally unsuited to one another in relationships that are bound to end in disaster. In very many of these situations the teenagers concerned simply don't want to know when family or friends try to warn them of the possible consequences. This is perfectly understandable. No one wants to be told what to do, especially teenagers, who have their whole lives ahead of them. They know that they will make mistakes, and if they are to learn to be independent-minded adults, they will learn life lessons from those mistakes.

At every age we need to learn from the mistakes we make. Before Sheena had that painful experience with Mike, I don't believe that anyone could have talked to her or warned her that he used women as sexual objects, or rather, to be more accurate, people could have talked, but she was not ready to listen. She didn't want to hear negative things about the man she believed she loved. Of course she was aware that he had the reputation of treating other girls badly, but she truly believed he had put all that behind him. When they tell you love is blind, believe them. Being in love causes chemical changes in the brain that really do make a person see their loved one with rose-tinted spectacles.

It would be wonderful if Sheena learned the painful lesson from her broken relationship with Mike that if a woman feels she must have sex to hold on to a boyfriend, she is not motivated by loving feelings. Her behaviour is manipulated by the fear of losing him. Every intelligent person should know that relationships that make one feel special bring a level of security into one's life.

Do you want a simple way to check whether you're in a healthy, loving relationship or in a lustful one? Be gentle with yourself. Before you begin, bear in mind that adolescents are often more in love with the idea of being in love than with the person. There's nothing wrong with that, as long as you don't make the mistake of allowing yourself to be sexually exploited because you think it's love.

Let's be really honest here and admit that lots of teenagers exploit each other sexually, for all sorts of reasons. I'm not judging them, because I really believe that everyone starts out with good intentions. We all set out to meet our own needs: that's a fact of life that few people acknowledge. On the other hand, it's rare for a person to set out maliciously to hurt another person. Occasionally we read in the papers of a person who has HIV, and to get revenge on society, deliberately sets out to infect other people. I hardly need to tell you that these people are mentally ill. The disease has distorted their way of looking at things.

OK, let's get back to the question of finding out if you're in a relationship that is healthy for you. Does the relationship make you feel:

- Anxious to please?
- Worried that you might say the wrong thing?
- Careful of what you say and how you say it?
- Fearful of upsetting your partner?
- Sensitive to your partner's moods?
- Concerned s/he will leave you for someone else?
- Convinced that it is normal to feel like this when you're in love?

I have good news and bad news for you. The bad news is that if I have described how you feel in your current relationship, it's probably not a healthy relationship for you. If you feel you have to keep a partner sweet all the time, that's not love, that's fear. The good news is that when you have the maturity to recognise that you deserve better and decide that you want to be yourself, you will be amazed at what lies ahead. When you have the internal conviction that you will not allow anyone to use you selfishly or treat you in a disrespectful way, everything changes for the better and you come into your own power. Something in you changes, and you draw to you people who will treat you well. I really do believe they pick it up from your body language.

The kind of love needed in a relationship that is healthy for both people is motivated by a desire to please the beloved and the security that you are accepted even if you don't. If you want it, you can have that kind of relationship, although you may have to learn new relationship skills to do so. Family upbringing has a big influence on the attitudes and expectations people bring to relationships. Believe me, you can have very different kinds of relationships to the ones you see modelled in your family, if you are prepared to work at learning how to change the way you relate. Sadly, hardly anyone wants to put in the necessary work. Most people prefer to settle for what they know, even when it means living with constant anxiety and fear. Always remember that a loving relationship isn't a controlling one.

NOT IN THE BUSHES!
Boys are less likely than girls to think it is important to be in love to have sex. Of course, they're aware that girls

want a relationship, and many are only too aware that women are looking for a commitment. Men and women are often looking to meet different needs when they are sexually intimate. Young men can have a very casual attitude to recreational sex. They're not fussy about where they have sex, and if we are truly honest, it's only fair to acknowledge that a tiny number care even less about who their partner is.

A fact of modern life that is obvious to anyone who studies the attitudes of young men is that there is no shortage of young women who are prepared to accept being treated as a sex object. There is an old adage that says, 'it takes two to tango'. It takes two to have sex, and there's no point in girls complaining that boys are only out for one thing and that few young guys know how to treat a girl right. The harsh truth is that while young women are prepared to have sex in the open, their male partners don't have to do anything to bring about change. Guys who don't mind having sex in the bushes or against a wall down a dark lane find willing partners. The practice would stop if girls demanded better and refused to have sex in uncomfortable surroundings.

CASUAL SEX

Peer pressure is highly influential and gives credibility to a damaging notion that many teenagers hold: the belief that sexual freedom means liberation from emotional involvement. The fact that this view is widely held doesn't mean it's correct. Some young people who are out for a good time see recreational sex with no strings attached as a desirable option. Others accept the more traditional belief that one should be in a committed relationship with a trusted partner before even considering sexual intimacy.

It is unfortunate that teenagers have inaccurate information and wrong beliefs. Some believe that sex is an overpowering emotion that drives a person to do things in an out-of-control way. They are wrong. Sex has far more to do with the brain than the genitals. Sexual feelings don't overpower anyone. Mixed information again creates confusion about what is normal behaviour, and young people are pulled in opposite directions. Some have sex because their peers put pressure on them. Others do it because they want to rebel against parents who tell them not to do it. There are others who think that sex is normal and can't understand why adults make it such a big deal.

Public awareness of the emotional damage done to teenagers who engage in sex too early is almost entirely limited to sensational newspaper headlines about eleven-year-old boys who father children and twelve-year-old girls who have babies. The influence that parents and the family background have on the attitudes and behaviour of these children is rarely explained or highlighted by the media. There is huge denial in our society about adolescents who are sexually active and in need of adult guidance.

SOME CRAZY BELIEFS

Many adults admit to feeling confused and uncertain about what is normal. In the not-too-distant past, people were told that masturbation led to madness, made people go blind and caused their hair to fall out. Of course, none of this is true but you still have many adults who learned that solo sex was wrong and harmful and who have never questioned those beliefs.

I know you'll find it hard to believe that older people who were brought up with these beliefs actually felt very concerned about washing their genital area. They thought sex was in some way dirty and that area of the body should not be touched. Can you imagine that caring parents believed that children should remain innocent and not be sullied by teaching them about reproduction? Girls who were not prepared were terrified out of their wits when their first period arrived.

This all probably sounds a bit crazy to you, but whether you are aware of it or not, it has affected your own attitudes to sex and relationships. If your grandparents held those beliefs about keeping children innocent, your mother and father probably didn't get any sex education, so you may be at a disadvantage. If you're lucky, your parents will have come into the real world and made some attempt to educate you. If your mother and father are like some parents, who say that what was good enough for them is good enough for you, they will leave you to fend for yourself and you will end up like the majority of peer-educated adolescents, with an enormous amount of information and no way of working out how much of it is correct.

Holistic Relationships
I think it is becoming clear that readiness for sex involves far more than feeling sexy and acting on those feelings. It involves not only your physical, but your social, emotional and spiritual well-being. It also involves how naive, innocent or worldly-wise you are. If you dream of

falling in love and living happily ever after, you're naive and still have the innocence to believe in fairy tales. If you have experienced being in love, you will realise how quickly your dream partner can make what used to seem boring into something that fascinates you. It's like you see it through their eyes and it becomes so different. Falling in love is wonderful: enjoy it, for it never, ever stays the same. Be prepared for change in a relationship that is healthy and growing. People who don't know this have unrealistic expectations of romantic relationships. Either these expectations change and they accept changes in the relationship, or they cling to what they had and it dies.

In the early stages of being in love, your brain chemistry changes and you are fine-tuned to see your beloved with rose-tinted spectacles. This blinkered stage could last two weeks, six months, two years or whatever. It never lasts and when the spectacles come off, cold reality shatters the illusion and makes a very different picture.

During the early 'in love' stage, each partner is loving and understanding. When they have an argument, both are prepared to apologise and forgive. In that early romantic phase, each partner is willing to make excuses when they are upset at a partner and give them the benefit of the doubt. When that early bloom of romance fades and reality hits, many relationships simply fall apart. Often couples go their separate ways, not because they don't love each other but because they haven't the skill to communicate about their differences without fighting. A fact of life that is not widely understood is that conflict stems from a failure to communicate with respect. Couples don't stop getting along because they don't talk enough. You probably already know that the reason is that they don't know how to listen in a way that shows they have heard and understood the other person's point of view.

When couples are willing to put work into their relationship, to develop the kind of honest, loving companionship where both feel valued and special, they move from the excitement of early romance into a love that continues to grow and strengthen. If they want to do this, they need to be able to share their thoughts and feelings and to do that, they need to build a respectful friendship. That kind of relationship takes effort to achieve.

The truth is that no couple has the energy to sustain the incredible high that comes with the early romantic feelings of being in love. They soar for a time and then drop to a plateau. The initial excitement wears off, as the deeper love that is needed to sustain a longer-term relationship emerges, or the couple break up.

Emotional Confusion

What most young people need is help to deal with those churning emotions that make them feel so elated and confused at the same time. It's great to read that you deserve to be treated with respect, but if you insist on looking for what you want, isn't there the possibility that you could be left on your own? That begs another question. Is it better to be happy without a partner than miserable in a relationship with one? If you're like many of the people with whom I work, you will probably tell me that you would prefer to settle for a little misery with a partner than have to face the world on your own. Hardly anyone ever seems to look to the future or to understand the consequences of staying in an unsatisfactory relationship.

You won't learn from your peers that when you feel that you need someone – anyone – you give away your power. Let me try to help you understand what you do to yourself. If I need a man in my life, I am trapped into keeping him sweet so that he will stay with me. He can then manipulate me into doing things I would prefer not to do. I will force myself to do whatever pleases him in order to hold on to him, and then, human nature being what it is, I will blame him for being insensitive to my needs.

The really major issue that few young people explore is why they are prepared to pay such a high price in misery in order to be part of a couple. If feeling low and miserable as a single is what they dread most, they are going to feel let down when they discover that no partner can ever do anything to change how a person feels. You're definitely not ready to be part of a relationship if you don't know that you are responsible for your own feelings. The person who thinks they want a partner usually needs to do a lot of work on self-esteem and self-image issues that will restore their self-confidence.

The blunt truth is that it's crazy to look to someone else for what you don't give to yourself. If you feel incomplete without a partner, it is a clear sign that you have personal issues to be resolved before you are ready for a healthy relationship.

5

SO THE EARTH MOVED?

JANE'S STORY

Seventeen-year-old Jane felt miserable as she waited for her boyfriend, Peter. She was madly in love with him. Although she told her friends that everything in their relationship was wonderful, she had to admit to herself that it wasn't. Her sex life was an utter disaster. She worried that perhaps she wasn't as sexy as her friends, and wished she knew what she could do to help her develop a stronger sex drive.

The truth was that sex with Peter wasn't at all what she had thought it would be. It was a terrible disappointment. He didn't know that, of course, because when they were having sex, she acted as if she was having a good time. Afterwards, she felt empty, disappointed and a little angry that she felt so frustrated. She was dissatisfied and she hated how she felt. Peter was her first lover. It was even more horrible that she didn't know where to turn for advice. Who could she talk to about feeling mixed up, frustrated and confused?

She wished she hadn't lied to her friends. They all believed that the earth moved every time she had sex with

Peter. There was no way she was going to tell the truth and admit that the earth stood still for her while Peter enjoyed a few pleasurable shudders. How could she tell anyone that she was relieved and disappointed when she felt Peter orgasm – relieved that she could now relax and stop pretending but disappointed because it had happened so quickly that she wasn't even fully turned on before it was all over.

Peter's Story

Peter was too inexperienced to know that Jane faked orgasms. When they had sex, he certainly enjoyed the thrills, but the truth was that after 'doing it' he felt as dissatisfied as he felt energised. Peter also had expectations of how sex should be that were not being fulfilled. For him, intercourse was awesome, an out-of-control explosion of shuddering pleasure that was over too quickly. He sensed that it was not as good for Jane as it was for him, but he never asked. He had heard that women didn't enjoy sex as much as men anyway. He wished he could find out if this was really true, but he hadn't a clue about where to go for the information. He certainly couldn't ask his mates.

One part of him wanted to be more in control of his body so that he could feel like a good lover. He longed to hold back his own orgasm until he had Jane squirming with pleasure. He liked to imagine her enjoying the heights of passionate desire, hungry for his body, but when he was with her, it was never as he had fantasised. He dreamed about being a great lover, giving Jane multiple orgasms, and worried that after such fantasies, he always masturbated. He felt uncomfortable once it was over, worried that he was getting addicted to satisfying himself.

He wasn't sure if solo sex was depriving him of the energy necessary to hold an erection and delay ejaculation. He had a vague recollection of a teacher in sex-education class who said that the danger of masturbation was that a guy got used to instant gratification and found himself unable to delay his own pleasure until his wife or partner was ready.

His sexually active male friends sounded like they were considerably better lovers than he was. He envied the boys who claimed they were enjoying earth-shattering experiences every time. He suspected that they were exaggerating, but he wasn't sure. He wasn't going to admit that sex for him was a disappointment, so he listened to his friends, pretended that his experiences mirrored theirs and boasted of sexual exploits that he had only enjoyed in his imagination and by his own hand.

It's Cool to Want It Hot

Jane and Peter are typical of many adolescents who engage in premarital sex. Like thousands of teenagers who are in love, they have a strong desire to communicate that love through passionate, erotic, fantastic sex, and nearly always fail to fulfil that aspiration. Sexually miseducated young people are rarely aware that such desires remain unfulfilled because they are unrealistic. They have crazy beliefs of how sex should be, so they boast to their peers that the earth moved, and their peers tell lies back and perpetuate the myths.

People of all ages have such daft expectations about sex and how it should make them feel that they seldom recognise how they are damaged by those unrealistic expectations. A person who aspires to a perfection that doesn't exist in real relationships is deluded, and bound to feel disappointed. To put it bluntly, many couples – without realising what they are doing – set themselves up to feel sexually inadequate because sex is not as hot and steamy as they think it should be. When they fail to measure up to some imagined standards, they can often feel depressed about their 'inadequate' sexual performance.

The great tragedy is that otherwise intelligent people seem to lose every shred of sense they ever had when it comes to seeking ecstatic satisfaction from sex. It's obvious that most adults, including those who are married, rarely question the sources from which they received their sex education. Even the most cursory analysis shows that sex is still a taboo subject in families. It is terrifying to see how much potentially damaging misinformation about sex and sexuality is widely accepted as fact. It's amazing how many college students believe that a girl can get pregnant only around the time of ovulation, or that once a man wears a condom he is protected from sexually transmitted diseases.

Don't Believe What You Hear

Researchers believe that most people who are asked about their private sex lives lie. Men and women tell different kinds of lies. Men are more likely to lie and say they have had sex when they haven't, or claim that they always bring a partner to climax. Many males still aspire to the status that comes from 'sowing their wild oats' with a wide variety of women. At one time, the guy who could 'make it' with lots of women was highly regarded. Today, that status is gone and he is more likely to be looked on with pity as a pathetic user of women.

Even though sexual equality has made many changes for the better, different standards of behaviour are still expected from women. Females also lie about having sex. They are more likely to deny they had it to protect their reputations. The girl who sleeps around and is known to have been with different men will be labelled a 'slut'. When you understand the double standards by which the sexes are judged, it's easy to see why some women feel it is better to be dishonest. A huge percentage of women admit to faking orgasm to make their partners feel good.

All this dishonesty breeds misinformation that leads to confusion and false beliefs. The truth is that nobody in the whole world can tell me, or you, or anyone else what we should be feeling when we have sex. Ignore everything you see on television or on videos. You know they are actors putting on an act. Dismiss everything you have heard about what is supposed to happen. What happens for other people is fine for them and it says nothing at all about what will make you happy or loved or sexually satisfied.

We simply don't have the language to describe any experience, never mind one as intimate as having sex. Let's see if I can help you grasp what I'm saying. There is no way that I can describe to you exactly what I am feeling so that you too can fully appreciate the experience

I am having. Suppose I tell a male friend, 'I feel sexy'. I might like to think he knows exactly what I mean, but I'd be wrong. No man can know exactly how a woman feels when her body responds sexually. He simply doesn't have the right equipment to understand her experience.

All of us use the words 'love' and 'like' to describe many very different kinds of feelings and relationships. When I tell my mother, my daughters, a male friend and a female friend that I love them, I am using the same words to describe totally different emotions. Each person hearing those words will make sense of them in a way that reflects their understanding of our relationship. When I use the words, 'I love you' to my male friend, I am talking about different feelings to those for my female friend, although I use identical words.

Let's try to apply that same thinking to what happens when people talk about sex. Ask yourself, 'What are descriptions like: "It was fabulous"; "It was fantastic, amazing, great"; "It was really hot", communicating?' They are descriptive words used to describe a personal experience, nothing more.

ILLUSIONS

People who say how fantastic their experiences were have perceptions that are valid for them, Unfortunately, descriptions of fantastic experiences create expectations that put both men and women under pressure to attain similar explosive pleasures. Sadly, many people seem to be blinded into believing that other peoples' sex lives are better and more exciting than their own. They get caught up in the make-believe they watch on television and in videos. They aspire to the experiences they see depicted on the screen, unaware of the hours of planning and complicated choreography that goes into creating the illusions that breed sexual fantasies in so many viewers. It is terrible that so many people mistake fantasy for reality. When couples set out with wrong information and unrealistic expectations of sex, they think they are missing out. They compare how they feel with how they *think* they should be feeling and end up disappointed and frustrated.

One reason that I decided to write this book is to correct the wrong information that people of all ages have picked up about how sex should be. So much pain and unnecessary distress can be eliminated when couples get real and learn to stop putting pressure on themselves to be something other than they are. Satisfying sex has far more to do with love and honest communication than with techniques and performance.

GET REAL

It's hard to believe that so many otherwise well-informed women and men are so sexually miseducated that they dismiss the normal thrills and achievable pleasures of lovemaking as inadequate and unexciting. Psychiatrist Robin Skynner had a liberal outlook on premarital sex in what might be termed the pre-AIDS times. He believed it was a good idea for young people to pair off with lots of different partners, provided it didn't go against their religion or the moral code they wanted to follow. He explained that it was important for them to get plenty of experience emotionally and – if it was acceptable to them – sexually.

He said, 'The sexual experience itself is about the most positive, powerful and moving experience we can have, short of the religious ecstasy which most of us will never know'. He also believed that sex is exciting and fulfilling only to the extent that we can let go, lose control and give ourselves over to the experience. For a person to have the freedom to let go like Dr Skynner suggests, they need to be in a relationship where there is a lot of trust.

Satisfying Sex Depends on How Good the Relationship Is

College student Gail was an avid reader of magazines that had advice columns. She had her favourite magazine in her schoolbag when she met Martin. It recommended an exciting sexual position, with movement-by-movement instructions. Her body tingled with desire as she pictured in her mind's eye the illustration, which explained how a couple could have intercourse with the woman lying on her back and the man crouching over her, with his weight on his hands and knees. It was rated a difficult position and in her heart of hearts she knew she would never do more than fantasise about that kind of exciting sex.

The only position Martin ever used was the missionary position, and even though that was the position the couple were supposed to start with, she knew she didn't have the guts to follow the instructions for how the woman could spice it up. Her body was flexible and athletic enough for the acrobatic manoeuvres required, but she lacked the freedom to try something different.

The instructions said that as the man was penetrating the vagina she should carefully lift one leg and inch it under him so that it was almost crossing over the other leg. Gail always felt excited when she read about different ways to spice up the tried-and-trusted missionary position. However, she had never tried any of them and I bet she would never get around to trying anything new with Martin. You can probably guess why. She was too shy. She didn't have the kind of open and honest relationship with him that would allow her to talk about her needs or desires.

Usually teenagers, college students and married couples who pretend to be having a better time than they really are having believe that they are acting out of consideration for their partner. They fail to understand that when anyone feels they need to keep silent and feel they cannot be honest, they are not in a loving relationship. People tell themselves they are doing the other person a favour, when in reality they are too fearful to speak up and admit that something is not right. It is difficult to admit that when you are not honest, your behaviour shows that you cannot be trusted.

Often, acting in a very considerate way, where the other person's needs are always put first, is not consideration at all but a cover-up for fear and insecurity. If I don't have the freedom to be honest in words and in deeds – because if I did, I might hurt your feelings or upset you – I am not free to be myself. If I have to control my behaviour to keep someone else happy, I allow them to control me.

The bottom line is that if a person feels afraid to be honest with a partner, either because they don't want to hurt the partner's feelings or they fear the person might get angry with them, they are allowing themselves to be manipulated, whether they recognise this or not. If Jane is afraid to tell Peter she needs to feel nurtured and cared for by him, she is depriving him of the information he needs to realise that he is not meeting her very real and natural needs.

If she opens up and is real, she will probably make it easier for him to be real too. Her honesty could help him get up the courage to tell her that he wants to be a better lover. When either person is honest and allows him or herself to be vulnerable, they are showing great trust. If they cover up the hidden fears under the guise of playing considerate lovers, they will create inhibitions to honesty that will destroy any chance of a relationship that involves really satisfying sex.

GOOD SEX NEEDS TRUST

Honest communication is vital for love to flourish and grow. When I know that you are truthful with me, I learn to trust you. If you lie to me, even if you think you are only telling little white lies or your motive is to protect me in some way, you are damaging that trust. When a woman feels she can't trust the promises her partner makes, no matter how much she is in love with him, she won't ever feel the safety and security that makes for nurturing and fully satisfying sex.

Sex is bound to be disappointing for any couple who are dishonest with each other. If the woman pretends to have wonderful climaxes, she is giving her partner a message that sex is great for her. No matter how good her intentions, the result will be negative. She will end up feeling frustrated, and at some level, she will question if he truly cares for her. If the practice continues over a long period of time, her dissatisfaction will grow. In these situations it is common for women to grow resentful and feel they are being used.

If the man is fooled into believing he is a great lover, he has no motivation to change the way he makes love. It is her own behaviour that causes her to lose out. When he is not aware that there is a problem, he sees no reason to do anything differently. When she leaves him in the dark about how sexually frustrated she feels, how can matters improve?

If Gail and Martin want to create a more sexually fulfilling relationship for themselves, the first thing they need to do is to talk more. Really satisfying sex that is passionate, erotic and sensuous usually happens when two people are comfortable in each other's company and have the freedom to be real and honest about their likes and dislikes. If the woman is acting the part of the satisfied lover and he senses that she is pretending so that he will feel good, he will probably be hurt and feel that she can't be trusted. If lovemaking is not all that he expected, there is a good chance that he will blame himself for an inadequate performance. When a couple can bring themselves to be honest and give feedback about what they enjoy, they learn to satisfy each other's real needs. It's as simple as saying something like, 'I like when you do that' or 'That feels so fantastic; I'd love if you continued to touch me there.'

Telling It Like It Is

There are numerous studies to show that sex is better in a committed, monogamous relationship. Whatever your views on marriage, there is a lot of evidence to show that married people have sex more often and are more satisfied with their sex lives than either couples having affairs or engaging in premarital sex. Studies in the United States show that better sex is a natural by-product of having a solid, loving relationship. The American National Survey of Families and Households conducted in 1992 polled 13,000 adults. Long-term monogamous couples reported overall higher emotional and physical satisfaction with their sex lives. Researchers found that they made love twice as often as singles in the same age group. Similar conclusions were reached by the Janus Report on *Sexual Behaviour and Sex in America*.

When a woman acts as if she is having a better time than she is in reality, there will be no pressure on her partner to become a better lover. Love alone will not solve a problem they never discuss. If she cannot bring herself to be more honest, she will remain stuck in a rut, hiding her disappointment at how unsatisfactory their sex life is. If he does not tell her he is also dissatisfied, she will assume that things are better for him than they are.

There are thousands of couples, many of whom are married or in long-term relationships, who pretend everything is wonderful in bed when it isn't. They live with feelings of sexual inadequacy because they don't talk about sex. The tragedy is that so few people understand that a lack of sexual satisfaction is a clear sign that a couple have communication problems. Good sex is not about measuring heights of ecstasy. It is about communicating in a way that makes a person feel so accepted, special and nurtured that they can relax, and in this state, it's natural to reach the ecstasy that can't be reached when there is tension.

Failing to enjoy sexual satisfaction says nothing about how sexy a person is. A disappointing sexual experience in no way suggests that a person has a low sex drive or is with someone who doesn't have the right techniques to turn a partner on. Disappointing sex is more likely to be indicative of a failure on the part of the couple to listen to each other than any deficiency in their lovemaking techniques. A person's ability to be a passionate lover and romantically adventurous is directly connected to his or her freedom to communicate honestly with a partner. Trust is needed for honest communication, both in and out of bed.

6

Performance Anxiety

Louise's Story

'My husband Danny says I never want to have sex. He just doesn't get it when I tell him that I want to make love and that I want more than just sex. For me there is a big difference. Lovemaking involves feeling special and valued, but he just doesn't get it. He keeps asking me what I want, but he never listens when I tell him. He comes home in the evening, hardly has a word to say to me, and then at bedtime he expects me to be as excited and ready for sex as he is. He complains when I explain that I don't feel close and makes out that it is just an excuse to avoid having sex. Although I ask him to talk to me because it helps me to feel close and intimate and I need that closeness, he doesn't understand. Sometimes he makes me feel that I'm a selfish bitch holding out on him.

'He has even insinuated that I was more interested in sex before we were married, and that I put on an act to trap him. He tells me that he loves me but that no man could live up to my expectations. I'm terrified that if we can't sort this out, he'll have an affair.'

DANNY'S STORY

'I don't understand my wife Louise at all,' Danny told the marriage counsellor. 'Before we were married, she was always wanting to make love. She wore sexy clothes and lacy underwear and was always randy. She was great fun to be with and I felt really lucky that she was my girlfriend and that we had such an exciting sex life.

'We've been married for five years now, and everything's changed. She's still romantic and sexy, but she rarely wants to have sex. Even when she does, I get the feeling that she doesn't really want to do it. She makes me sound like I'm a sex fiend. I love her but we can't go on like this. Nothing I do is right for her.

'I blame all that pop psychology she's always reading. She talks about "making our relationship work" and how important it is to "keep our love life vibrant". You'd think that she would want to make love more often, but the opposite is the case. Since she started reading all this stuff, what I do in bed isn't good enough. She wants to communicate before we make love and expects all this foreplay stuff. Now she wants the right atmosphere and tells me that part of proper foreplay is to make her feel valued and special. I don't know how to make her feel that way.

'I don't know whether to believe that she used to fake it before or else she doesn't really love me because she certainly doesn't care about what I want. It's always "not tonight, dear", and I'm so frustrated and anxious. She makes it very clear that the way we have sex is not satisfying her or meeting her needs. My performance is not measuring up to her high and mighty expectations.'

What Do People Do in Bed?

It's almost impossible to get accurate information about what people do in bed. Why? The plain unvarnished truth is that people lie about their sexual exploits. One magazine found that 92 per cent of women surveyed admitted to faking orgasm at least once in their lives. It's hardly surprising that 40 per cent of the men questioned said they suspected that women have faked orgasm with them. Another 40 per cent weren't sure, and an amazing 20 per cent were prepared to swear that they gave their partner an orgasm every time.

You don't have to be a mathematician to work out that people can't be trusted when they talk about their sex lives. However we try to put a good spin on it, we have to admit that there is clear evidence to show that people of all ages lie about sex. Twelve-year-old boys lie and claim have to kissed half the girls in their neighbourhood because they want to feel cool. It's not acceptable for girls of the same age to boast about having lots of boyfriends. Even at that tender age, girls are expected to be loyal.

That loyalty extends from saying your boyfriend is a good kisser when you are twelve to claiming he is a great lover at twenty. A significant number of women choose to fake an orgasm and you don't have to be an Einstein to understand what their reasons are. A surprising number feel sexually inadequate and blame themselves. They fear that failure to reach a spine-tingling orgasm reflects badly on their sexuality. It must mean they have a low sex drive or lack the sexual responsiveness that drives men wild. Some have an inkling that their partner may not be a very sensitive lover, but fear that a man would be so hurt to learn this that he couldn't handle the truth and the relationship would be damaged. So they remain loyal and fake it in the mistaken belief that 'a wise woman fakes it until she makes it'.

Most women prefer to pretend to get great enjoyment from unsatisfactory sex than upset a partner. They would rather flatter the male ego than admit that the sexual experience was unsatisfactory. Others still blame themselves. They worry that failure to reach 'the big O' indicates that they need more sexual experience and if they could only get the right position or find better sexual techniques, they would discover the peaks of pleasure they so desperately desire.

Many of the 'How to Enjoy Ecstatic Sex' magazine articles and books are avidly read by women. They breed unrealistic expectations that men will have the stamina to have sex all night and bring their partners to unbelievable heights of pleasure. Hardly any readers write in to say what everyone with a grey cell in their head knows. Spending the night having sex is a fantasy for which almost no one has the stamina, not even on holidays. Research shows that a good relationship is necessary for good sex, but if readers write in to say this, their letters are not published.

The athletic prowess demanded for many of the sexual positions recommended for the most intense pleasure are unattainable by anyone other than a highly flexible gymnast. Magazines write about sex as if the simple positions that are within the ability of most ordinary folk to achieve are dull and boring. The tragedy is that so many people buy into the idea of improving their sex lives, without realising that the honest communication that is born in trust and love is the most potent aphrodisiac. Disillusioned teenagers who don't know any better are buying into beliefs that make them feel sexually inadequate

SEXUAL PERFORMANCE

There is no denying that people are vulnerable about their sexual performance. The problem for a person who sets out to have the earth move when they have sex is that they are putting sexual pressure on themselves. This pressure causes stress and is damaging to self-esteem. Poor self-esteem leads to an erosion in self-confidence. There is an old saying that you can fool some of the people some of the time but you can't fool all of the people all of the time. It's time for people of all ages to wake up to the myths and stop putting themselves under pressure. One reason why people have such unrealistic expectations about sex is they are bombarded with mixed messages about how it should be and have almost no accurate information to contradict the exaggerations that are put forward as the norm.

If you are like most people, you probably have a great deal more information about the physical than about the emotional and spiritual aspects of sex. You are probably fairly sure that some of what you heard about sex when you were growing up and about what people do to each other is crazy but you don't know how to check this out. For example, teenagers are often upset to hear that no one knows what causes homosexuality, but that everyone has some degree of it in him or her. They say this isn't true of them, but they rarely ask for a definition of homosexuality. Be careful. Ask for an explanation and check things out before you make assumptions about what people mean. If you talk to your friends, there's a good chance that they will have heard the same as you and you are left with half-truths and suspect information that you have no way of checking out.

Another sensitive topic that causes a great deal of embarrassment and is hard to ask questions about is masturbation. Until the last century, it was believed that semen contained little babies, and because scientists had this wrong belief, solo sex was viewed as the killing of unborn babies. People were taught that wasting sperm was as morally serious as an act of murder. To stop adolescents from masturbating, they were told that their hair would fall out or that they would go crazy. A lot of the confusion and guilt that still surrounds masturbation comes from ignorance, but that's not a great deal of help to you if you're not sure how to find the facts.

You are likely to have wrong information about the sex lives of adults, especially your parents. Most young people find it hard to imagine that their parents and grandparents have a sex life. Children can accept that their mum and dad had sex at least once, because they are alive. But the idea of parents having fun in bed doesn't bear thinking about for lots of young people. Of course, the same head-in-the-sand attitude is mirrored by parents, who may accept that other people's teenagers are sexually active, but are in total denial about their own. They simply cannot conceive of their child having sex.

WHY ARE YOU PLANNING TO HAVE SEX?

Very few of us have enough insight into how we think and feel to give an honest reply to the question 'Why do you intend to have sex?'. Sex is an instinct that is as powerful as the instinct for food and drink. That's one reason why it is illegal to have under-age sex. Governments and health departments are only too aware of the very serious long-term consequences of premature sexual activity. The laws about statutory rape are there to protect young people from themselves.

It is only honest to admit that many people of all ages have sex without giving any thought to the consequences and they claim to have a good time. Recent studies suggest that when people grow up and become more mature, they often regret their sexual past. In hindsight, they wish that they had been more selective about who they went to bed with, and the majority think they would have been better off if they had waited.

Not all couples have sex in order to meet their intimacy needs and share their love. When sex is misused, it does not bring a sense of closeness or fulfilment. Some men and women are simply out to have a good time and they do not have any sense of a need for love or commitment before they make for the bedroom. They have sex rather than make love, and afterwards, they may ask themselves: 'Is that all there is to it?'

Young men who selfishly use a person to enjoy sexual thrills usually find the experience a disappointment. The ecstasy that connects a couple and brings that sense of oneness that makes sex so fulfilling and joyful for couples in relationships is rarely experienced unless there is commitment and love on both sides. When one person is in love and their feelings are not reciprocated, sex is not a bonding experience.

A more telling question than 'Why are you planning to have sex?' is 'For what purpose do you intend to have sex?' I expect you might reply that people have sex for reproduction, to make babies, for pleasure. You might even suggest they do so to make a partner fall in love, and we both know that this is a crazy reason to have sex – although one that is very common.

How Accurate Are Your Sources of Information?
We learn from our parents and our Church. We watch television and videos. We read about sex in magazines and books. A fact of life is that most of us have been given incorrect or inaccurate information. We do not go through life unaffected by what we see and read. Sexual imagery has an effect and the reality is that it influences us to have fantasies about sex. There is a world of difference between fantasising about sex with different people and engaging in sex with different partners. Multiple partners bring a greater risk of sexually transmitted infections.

You may scorn the idea of monogamous sex within marriage as old-fashioned and out of date. I cannot argue with you if you tell me that only a hypocrite would suggest that everyone who is married is happy and faithful to their spouse. Of course they're not. Marriage breakdown happens all the time. Yet it must meet human needs, as many people remarry after a divorce and even if their second relationship breaks down, they go for it a third time.

Television talk show hostess Oprah Winfrey presented some programmes on 'Rescuing Marriage' with Dr Phil McGraw, who had been married to the same woman for twenty-three years. In her introduction she said Phil was different to many of the other relationship experts she had had on her programmes over the years. Some of them had been married two and three times. She was so right. Our relationships are as good as our communication and relationships where there is good communication seldom have conflict issues that cannot be resolved. Talking is never the problem. People tend to talk too much. The real problem is that they don't know how to listen. Relationships get into difficulties because people have never learned to listen beyond the words to pick up their partners' feelings.

Good sex involves listening for feelings. If a person doesn't have an intimate friendship with a sexual partner, how can sex be great? What makes having casual sex so potentially damaging to self-esteem is the lack of intimacy. Anyone who argues that you can be intimate with a stranger doesn't understand what s/he is saying. The failure of sexual partners to talk is potentially downright dangerous.

Dissatisfied with Sex?

Many, many sexually active people are dissatisfied with their sex lives. They are not getting the pleasurable experiences they anticipated from sex. Some want to know what they can do to make it better. Many married people who are in a loving relationship would like to get this incredibly important information without acknowledging that they need it.

It's very common for people who are out for a good time to compare their experiences with what they think is happening for their friends. The belief that others are having a far better time is widespread. As you know, one of the reasons why so many people are screwed up about sex is because of dishonesty and lies. The majority of men are poorly informed about foreplay and believe many of the macho myths.

GUILT

Why do so many people feel guilty about their sexual behaviour? Most young people are influenced by the traditional belief that sex should be saved for marriage, even when they reject it. It is widely accepted today that if you love someone, it is OK to have sex, provided you act responsibly and use protection. But even though many consider the wait-until-marriage belief old-fashioned and out-of-date, it doesn't stop guilt feelings coming up and causing discomfort for them.

Our family values are the rules we live by. They are very deeply ingrained in us. Without our being aware of it, they have a powerful influence on how we live our lives. It's as if we carry within us a rule book setting out expectations of our parents, teachers, church and society. When we fail to live up to the rules or meet the expectations we believe people have of us – and this could include a teacher you had in junior school that you haven't seen in a decade – we feel bad. The kind of guilty feelings that shame us are an inappropriate response to a perceived failure to live up to another person's expectations of how we should be. Guilt and shame are ways in which we punish ourselves with negative feelings when we don't measure up.

It is important for you to understand that you develop patterns of relating as an adult that are similar to the ways you learned to relate as a child. Imagine you grew up in a tactile family where there was a friendly atmosphere and you were hugged regularly. Then you would be very used to physical affection. You would feel very comfortable with affectionate intimacy. You would find it easy to touch someone in appropriate ways or to be close to them without that proximity making you feel sexy.

If you were reared in a non-tactile family in which your parents were not getting along and where love, nurturing and intimacy were in short supply, it would be a very different story. If you didn't grow up with physical affection, you would have a different attitude to intimate male/female relationships. This is why some people feel very comfortable with intimate gestures that others view with mistrust and suspicion. If you find it hard to believe that a person can enjoy a loving, physically affectionate relationship without it leading on to full sex, you probably grew up in a non-tactile family.

Playing a Role

We all want to feel loved and accepted for who we are. If you feel that you cannot be really yourself with your partner, be wary. When you are not free to be yourself, you are not free to enjoy intimacy and you are cutting yourself off from relationship. When you do not feel confident enough with your partner to let her see who you really are, what you are doing is acting out a role. We all do this to some degree, in order to protect ourselves from getting hurt. When I act a role, you do not see me, you see only the image I convey to you in my role-play. If you feel you have to do this with a partner, then having sex is more likely to have you end up feeling more lonely than fulfilled or connected.

CONFUSING LUST WITH LOVE

It is hard to distinguish between the need to have one's sexual identity affirmed and the need for nurturing and affection. Sex for men is frequently linked to the male need to prove his masculinity. A person's need for closeness, intimacy and love is often confused with sexual needs. It is highly likely that the experience of strong sexual desires will be strongly influenced by a combination of all of these feelings. It would be foolish to believe that sexual desire is a signal that the body is simply crying out for genital sex. The desire to fulfil your intimacy needs for closeness, self-acceptance and sexual identity may feel like a powerful desire for genital sex. This is one reason why basing a decision on feeling ready to have sex is not such a good idea. It is easy to confuse wants, desires and needs. Many young people have strong views on monogamy. Even when they do not consider that marriage is an option for them, they expect a partner to be faithful.

Having a good body or knowing the physical techniques to turn on a partner is not nearly as important for a wonderful sex life as many people believe. Unfortunately, people are confused by contradictory information.

Most of us get our facts from different sources that promote very different values. Our parents, religion, teachers, friends and the media all give us information. You wouldn't need to be a genius to work that these sources have different agendas or viewpoints. They offer the information that confirms what they believe, and the end result is that teenagers and young adults are pulled in different directions when trying to decide what to do.

As a young child, you have to rely on your parents for advice on what is best to do or how to behave. Sadly, many teenagers rebel against such advice and decide to go their own way. Hardly any adolescents who have sex have the freedom to be open and honest with their parents. They need to talk to someone, so they tell their peers about having a good time. No teenager sets out to put pressure on others to have sex, but that is often the result. Peer pressure is one of the most commonly cited reasons why teenage boys have sex.

Before trying to find out whether you are ready to have sex or not, it is more logical to begin by exploring why you want to have sex. This is not an easy question. To give an honest answer, you will need to think holistically about your physical, emotional, and spiritual wellbeing. What you have learned about sex from the earliest days of life will have a strong influence on your thinking and, most especially, how you feel about yourself as a sexual person.

OUT FOR A GOOD TIME

We have to acknowledge that there are people of all ages who are just out for a good time and see nothing wrong with one-night stands. Every adult in the country should know the physical dangers of engaging in unprotected sex and the risks of contracting sexually transmitted diseases. Most of us are not well educated about how potentially damaging emotionally it is to have sex in the absence of a loving relationship. By now you may have learned that the most erotic, intense and fulfilling sex is enjoyed within a committed long-term relationship like marriage. This is part of most religious and spiritual traditions.

Teenage romance is often based on lust rather than love. If you make a mistake and have sex with the wrong partner, you will have to live with the consequences for a very long time. It is difficult to convince college students that although they have strong sexual feelings, they haven't the emotional maturity to deal with the strong desires that acting on those powerful hormonal feelings will arouse. I know it's not a very romantic approach, but you need to be honest more than you need to be spontaneous. Rather than base your decision to have sex on when you feel ready, ask yourself 'How do I know if I am in love or in lust?'

7

THERE ARE SIX IN THE BED – AND IT'S NOT AN ORGY!

DIANE'S STORY

'The only time Grandad knows what he feels is when he gets angry,' complained Diane to her mother Julie, 'and Dad is no better. He's a right chip off the old block. When he gets mad, he really blows his top and we all know that he is angry. That's the only time I am ever sure that he really feels anything. I'm not going to let my son grow up like that and be out of tune with his feelings. I don't want Matthew denying his feelings or suppressing them, and I certainly don't want him to be teased in this family or called a wimp. It's natural for a child to cry when he is hurt. It's not unmanly, and if Dad doesn't stop telling him that only girls cry, I'll have to think seriously about whether I can let him stay here when I'm not with him.'

Julie had never seen Diane so assertive before and she understood why. Her son-in-law, Mark, was a sensitive man who wasn't afraid to show his emotions, and his son, Matthew, was like him. Her own husband hated any display of emotion. If she cried when watching a sad video, he just laughed at her and said she was crazy to cry over a soppy film. She knew he didn't really mean to be harsh with the child. He was just doing what all the macho men in his family did.

She could see where he learned to be like that – he was exactly like his father. He even sounded like Grandad at times.

SIX IN THE BED

I had better explain immediately what I mean by 'There Are Six in the Bed'. Of course, I'm not thinking of six people physically getting into bed together. I'm not suggesting that anyone has an orgy. What I want you to understand is that you cannot get away from the influence of your parents. Whether you lived with your mum and dad, or one of your parents was absent, they have a powerful influence on how you think and what you feel and believe. When you become part of a couple, you bring your parents into the relationship.

One way to alert you to just how powerfully you are influenced by your parents is to get you to picture six in the bed. It is almost as if, when a woman gets into bed, she brings her mum and dad with her, inside her head. When her partner gets into bed, he also brings the mother and father that are in his head with him. That's a vitally important piece of information for anyone who is thinking of having a sexual relationship. Why? You will judge any relationship you have by comparing it to what your parents had.

The need to feel loved is strong in all of us. Whether you come from a happy or unhappy family, you have beliefs about what it means to love and be loved. Did you know that the basic personality is formed in the first seven years of life? The emotional damage that we suffer during those early years remains with us for life.

As the psychologist and priest John Powell SJ says, 'We are very largely shaped by others, who, in a most frightening way, hold our destiny in their hands. We are, each of us, the product of those who have loved us or refused to love us.' Psychologists pay a great deal of attention to family relationships. Children learn how to feel loved in their first intimate experiences with parents. Those early experiences play a vitally important role in how a person learns to form and maintain affectionate attachments throughout life.

How you feel about yourself is powerfully influenced by how nurturing your parents were. As adults, we seek out emotional situations similar to those we experienced in childhood. So let's say that both your parents worked and as a child you didn't get a lot of attention. You are used to being ignored, so you unconsciously choose partners who don't give you a lot of attention. The theory is that you seek out people and situations that bring up the feelings you are used to, and even when you plan to do the opposite and set out to give yourself what was missing, the chances are that you are unlikely to succeed.

Psychologist Tracey Cox gives a lovely example of how the parents we carry in our head influence us. 'Say your parents were cruel or unloving. You'll tend to seek out men who are equally callous and try your hardest to make them love you. If they love you, somehow it makes up for Mum and Dad not loving you, because in the murky bits of your brain, they are Mum and Dad'. She goes on to explain that you don't realise what you are doing when you try to get the love that you needed from your parents from this man. In other words, everyone brings emotional baggage from childhood and from past relationships with them, wherever they go.

WE ACT LIKE OUR PARENTS

As children, we learn to relate and communicate by watching our parents. They are the role models that we look to and learn from. If, when you were young, they spoke to each other pleasantly and treated people with respect, you will have observed positive body language and respectful communication. Without being aware of it, you will have learned healthy communication skills. A child who is treated with respect grows up with positive messages which create good self-esteem.

If your adult carers fought, were sarcastic, put others down, were nice to people face-to-face and horrible behind their backs, you come from a very normal family with poor relationship skills. If you want your adult relationships to be kinder and more sensitive, they can be. You can learn to relate differently, but it will take a lot of work and effort to develop different relationship skills.

I believe that my parents did not have a happy marriage. Some of my family think it is incredibly disloyal of me to let my parents down by putting this in a book. As a teenager, I swore that I wouldn't marry. I had two very serious relationships with boyfriends who wanted to marry me, but as soon as the relationships got to that stage I got cold feet and backed off. The first time my husband asked me to marry him, I was upset and asked him why he wanted to spoil a lovely friendship. He said, 'Marriage doesn't spoil friendships, people do. If you marry me, we can have any sort of relationship we want.' He was right. We are still friends, and over thirty years later, we are still happily married to each other.

When parents don't get along, they make life a misery for themselves and for their children. Perhaps I had better clarify what I mean. If they are angry, bitter and resentful towards each other, their children suffer. If you were unfortunate enough to grow up in a family where your mother and father had problems in their relationship, if they showed little or no emotional support for each other, it puts you at a big disadvantage. You learn to relate in emotionally unhealthy ways. As an adult, you will have unrealistic expectations about how love should be. You will find it more difficult to recognise emotionally abusive behaviour. Occasionally you find parents who feel perfectly comfortable in their own relationship. They have an agreement that they can say whatever they like to each other, and whatever mechanism they have for filtering hurt out of nasty statements works very well for them. For their children or friends, it can be a nightmare to be around the constant bickering.

Whether you come from a loving or troubled family, you have already learned very important lessons about the kind of adult relationships you want. Most young adults who are thinking about what they want in a relationship will discover that they would like some things to be the way they were with their parents, and other things to be totally different. Many teenagers who grow up with parents who have serious problems like alcoholism, physical violence or emotionally abusive behaviour, swear that when they grow up, things will be different for them. They will never behave like that parent.

Unhappily, many go on to repeat the mistakes of their parents. They act out what they saw happening in their childhood, because that is what people do. They model themselves on how they see their parents treat each other. They become their parents.

If you are interested in a serious long-term relationship you need to find out what your partner's family is like. Don't be terribly surprised if you discover that they remind you of your own.

Do You Want to Marry a Man Like Your Dad?

We can't avoid picking up some of our parents' attitudes to sex and relationships. The family therapist Virginia Satir says, 'Much is shown the growing child about himself as a sexual being in his home by the way the parents treat each other and how openly and frankly they can deal with male and female sexual matters. If you, as a woman, do not appreciate and find joy and pleasure in your husband's body, how can you teach your daughter an appreciation of men? The same is true for the father.'

Are you familiar with the old saying that women who love their fathers marry a man just like their dear old dad? Well, there's a lot of truth in it. Falling in love is about a great deal more than sexual attraction. There is a very obvious chemistry between people who are in love that cannot be fully explained. Psychologists take a great deal of the romance away when they suggest that the reason we are sexually attracted to someone is because they are similar to us in a psychological sense.

The most dramatic proof for this theory is an exercise called the family systems exercise, which is designed to demonstrate how couples who are strangers pick each other out. Psychiatrist Robin Skynner said this exercise demonstrated for him more clearly than he had ever realised how unconscious attraction works.

People who do not know each other, ideally complete strangers, come together without talking. They are asked to choose a person from the group, in silence, who either reminds them of someone in their family or gives them the feeling that they would have filled a gap in the family. Without speaking, they move around and look at the others. When they pick a partner, they are invited to talk, to see if they can discover why they chose each other. They are encouraged to share about their family backgrounds.

Then each couple is asked to choose another couple to make a foursome. This small group is asked to form itself into a family, agreeing with each other which role each person will take. Then they share what was in their family background that led to their decision.

The final part of the exercise is that each group gives feedback, and when they do, people invariably discover that they chose others whose families functioned like their own. Perhaps they all had absent fathers when they were young, or came from families who didn't show affection, or all their families suffered some big loss. What convinced Skynner that something extraordinary was going on was that the first time he used this exercise, he was worried that the people who were last to be picked would feel like rejects, so when he was taking the feedback, he put off asking them until the very end. They were fascinated with the result, because they had all been fostered or adopted or brought up in children's homes. They had all felt rejected early in life, and in some mysterious way, they sensed this and unerringly picked each other out.

Whether you are happy to hear this or not, there is a lot of evidence to support the idea that couples unconsciously choose each other because of similarities in childhood experiences and specific family problems. If you're a woman, the way you feel about your father affects how you feel about all men. If you're a man, it's the other way around. If you want a relationship that mirrors what your parents have, count yourself lucky. If you look at your parents and want a relationship like theirs for yourself, you don't have to do anything, because in all likelihood, you will act out with your life partner what you saw acted out in your family. If you want a very different kind of relationship, you can have it, but you are going to have to do a lot of work.

Do You Want to Marry A Woman Like Your Mum?

If you have happily married parents who love each other, or parents who separated, or had affairs, or you come from a single-parent family where Mum has brought you up on her own and you never see your father, it will have a bearing on the kind of adult relationships you will want. You can do nothing to change what happened to you as a child. What you can do is to understand that you are powerfully influenced by how you saw your parents relate and as an adult you are likely to treat your partner or spouse the way you saw your mother and father treat each other. If you want your relationships to be different, and very many people do, then you need to hold on to what your parents had that you want for your own relationships and discard the behaviours and responses you don't want in your life.

That is never easy to do because history tends to repeat itself, particularly family history. No matter how much our parents love us and want to do their best for us, they make mistakes and we get emotionally damaged. How your grandparents brought up your mother and father influences the way that they in turn reared you. Ideally, Mum and Dad love each other and are affectionate, sensitive people of integrity who get on well with everyone in their family. For most families, the picture is like that only some of the time. For others, it has never at any time been like that; they have never felt loved or special in their whole life.

Are you familiar with the old saying that a boy who loves his mother will look for a wife like her? Well there's a lot of truth in it. Think about how your dad treats your mum. If he treats her like a queen, that is how you will treat women. If he has cheated on your mum, you will have learned that men can need 'a bit on the side'. If Mum is independent and does her own thing, you will have the expectation that this is how women should be. I'm sure you have the idea. People treat their partners or spouses the way they saw their parents treat each other, unless they decide to do otherwise.

Can You Stop History Repeating Itself?

A good way to predict what kind of adult relationships you are likely to have is to look at how both sets of parents relate. If his parents have stayed together and have a warm, loving relationship, it is likely that he has the skills to create a similar relationship for you. If they make each other miserable but would never dream of separating, you could end up settling for a miserable existence, unless you break the cycle and develop a more positive way of relating.

If your parents are happily married and still love each other, you can be 100 per cent certain that they talk to each other and have a sense of humour. You have a good chance of creating a loving relationship that will last because that is what was modelled for you. If your parents had problems and separated, or cheated on each other, be prepared to acknowledge that you have a higher risk of being unfaithful or leaving a partner when the going gets rough.

There is no doubt that it is more difficult to find and keep an exclusive long-term relationship like marriage today. Infidelity is more common than most of us would like to admit. Until very recently, a man could not prove paternity. He had to believe his wife when she said he was the father of their children. DNA testing has changed that forever, and more and more men are discovering that their wives cheat with other men and that they did not father children they were told were theirs. If your mother was unfaithful, she showed you that women play around, and if that is part of your belief system, you may find it hard to trust women.

By now you will understand that, too often, the mistakes of the parents are passed down and repeated from generation to generation unless the cycle is broken. Believe me when I tell you that the first step in breaking the cycle is to learn to be aware of the positive and negative relationship skills that you bring with you from your family of origin. If they are not working for you, discard them and learn new ones. The key to having the relationship you want is communication. Your relationships will be as loving and deep as your communication.

What Did Your Parents Teach You About Love?

Parents teach children how they want them to behave by giving or withholding love and children need that love so badly that they learn to think, act and feel in ways that meet with parental approval. Almost from the moment of birth, children learn about gender and whether it is good to be a boy or girl. Men and women develop different relationship skills, so it's hardly surprising that they do not understand love in the same way.

It gets even more complex when you take personal likes and dislikes into account. What makes one woman feel really loved and special may be a turn-off for another. Intimacy that meets the emotional needs of one man may send another running for shelter to escape being engulfed. What makes you feel loved at one time in your life may not fulfil you at another.

I cannot define what love means or spell out what it means to feel loved. Only you know what will fulfil your emotional and sexual needs. It's easier to say what love is not than what it is. It is certainly a feeling, which is something you already know. Frequently it is confused with lust. You don't have to be worldlywise to know that the three little words 'I love you' are frequently said when what is meant is 'I want to have sex with you.'

Young guys think about sex all the time. They lust after girls, and many – but not all – will have sex whenever, and with whoever is willing. I know this is a generalisation and some guys are saving themselves for the right relationship. Young women, on the other hand, think less about sex and more about love, and meeting a man who will be faithful. This is not because women don't enjoy sex; it's because they want a man who has sex with them to love them only. They are looking for a committed relationship, as early as the first date.

Guys need to be aware of the five recognised stages of commitment. From day one, women nearly always want to be part of a couple, while he is happy to be uncommitted and free. For women, love and commitment are interwoven. This is as true of a ten-year-old girl who kisses a young lad who only comes up to her shoulder as it is of a twenty-year-old woman who is having sex. Women see themselves as part of a couple before a man even realises that she expects him to be faithful to her.

Stage 1	The desire to see him again.
Stage 2	She is happy to commit and be faithful to him.
Stage 3	She wants him to know that he is the special one.
Stage 4	She is dropping hints that she would like them to be together.
Stage 5	She wants their couple status to be publicly recognised.

There is a widespread expectation in our society that effective relationship and sexuality education programmes will teach teenagers about loving relationships and about fertility control, which should have the effect of preventing teenagers getting pregnant. Programmes teach young people about 'safe sex' practices and how to use contraception, but there is evidence to show that they fail to have any impact on sexual behaviour. Why? I believe it is because none of the policy makers involved have the courage and conviction to begin with what is taught by the primary educators, the parents.

In no other school subject are the basics that the child has been taught ignored. It's all very wonderful to aspire to teach children about loving relationships – what a beautiful sentiment – but in practical terms, what children and adolescents and college students and teachers understand by love reflects what they learned about loving and being loved from their families. Their culture, religion and the media and wider society influence thinking, but the first and most influential teachers are the parents.

Young prople must experience loving family relationships for healthy emotional development and in order to develop good self-esteem. When children are deprived of a loving family, the foundations on which they base their expectations of adult relationships are suspect.

Love cannot be defined in words because there is no language that can accurately define an experience. The relationship and sexuality programmes with which I am familiar ignore the impact of dysfunctional family relationships, so it's as if teachers are using a foreign language to children from dysfunctional backgrounds when they discuss loving and being loved. Although it is widely recognised that the way teenagers are parented has a bearing on how early they become sexually active and how sexually responsible they are when they do, this information is seldom acknowledged.

Let's be honest and spell it out. Students everywhere are denied the education that would give them the training, understanding and direction they need to have healthy, nurturing relationships that make them feel loved and special. While teachers are reluctant to face reality and acknowledge how the attitudes and values of parents impact on teenage sexual behaviour, the number of teenage pregnancies is unlikely to fall.

Students don't learn in a vacuum; they bring their personal experiences of how they were loved to bear on what they are taught about loving relationships. How is it possible to teach girls and boys about love, or to give them realistic expectations of what it means to look for respect from a partner, if they come from an abusive or violent family where adults have no respect for each other, and the influence of the parents' relationship is ignored? To inform, encourage or mature the relational, emotional and sexual lives of teenagers in our western society, we have to acknowledge the impact of how a child is parented.

We have seen that the state of their parents' relationship is a big factor in whether or not young people feel loved. Whether their partents are married, single or separated has an impact. Every expectation you have about how you want to be loved by a partner is coloured by the relationships within your own family. If your parents love each other and enjoy a warm, physically affectionate partnership, you are indeed a lucky person. You have grown up with role models that have taught you important lessons about how to be affectionate and to give and receive love. If you didn't have that and your parents don't get along, you probably need to re-examine the beliefs you have about love. A little soul-searching will show where you have distorted thinking.

Some of what our parents teach us about relationships is learned when we are too young to question and investigate what we are told or have observed. I regularly meet students who fall madly in love with partner after partner who treats them badly. They put it down to bad luck. I put it down to making bad choices that are influenced by wrong information. They are subconsciously choosing people who treat them badly because that is what they saw modelled in their family.

It is very difficult to admit to yourself that you have wrong ideas about what love is. It's hard to admit that you pick partners who make you miserable and to acknowledge that they give you what you are looking for when they treat you badly – when they treat you the way you got used to your family treating you.

There is a strong family loyalty that stops people telling the truth about parents who fought or were neglectful, abusive, manipulative or incestuous. If that describes your background and you fail to acknowledge the problems in your family of origin, you are at high risk of having history repeat itself. When you deny, ignore or push away the pain, it doesn't disappear. It remains hidden or repressed in you and you will subconsciously seek to repeat those patterns.

Anyone who claims to have had an idyllic childhood with adoring parents who were sensitive to their every need and never for one moment upset them is either lying or living a fantasy. The bottom line is that even the best-intentioned and most loving parents cause hurt and emotional damage. It took me a long time to acknowledge that while I was doing the best I could to be a loving mother, I often said or did things that did emotional damage and hurt my children. I'm still trying to learn that where showing love is concerned, actions speak louder than words. So much unnecessary pain and suffering is caused by good people who intend to show love by their actions and mess up because they fail to communicate their goodwill.

So many relationship problems begin when one person thinks they are doing something loving that will please the other but they don't get around to saying that that is their intention. They go right ahead, expecting a positive response. Then, when their loved one doesn't respond with delight, they are disappointed and that disappointment pushes them apart. It's not the disappointment but the failure to talk about it and hear how the other person feels that creates the sense of growing apart.

A very famous example is that of the couple who were having marital problems and were seeing a counsellor. She sent them away to do something nice for each other. At their next appointment, the wife was very angry and accused her husband of not doing what was asked. He vehemently denied this. When the counsellor asked, 'What did you do for your wife?' he explained that he got up early on Saturday morning, went out and washed, waxed and polished their car.

The therapist was a woman and she felt as puzzled as the wife, so she asked, 'Why did you this for her?' He explained, 'She likes the car to look well.' The poor fellow believed that he was putting in all that work and effort to please his wife and it had the opposite effect. She was angry and displeased. It acted to drive a wedge between them until he explained.

This is a great example of how the failure to communicate leads to misunderstandings that can make actions that are intended to show love feel and appear selfish and create distance rather than the intended closeness. There is just one guaranteed way to avoid such problems: learn to communicate openly and honestly.

8

Contraception

James's Story
James knew he was in trouble as soon as he remembered that he had left a condom in the jeans he had asked his mother to wash. She was bound to check the pockets before she put the jeans in the washing machine and he guessed that as soon as he got home from work his mother would freak. She didn't approve of Sharon, his girlfriend. Even though he was seventeen, she said he was too young to be in a relationship. She blamed Sharon for distracting him from the work he needed to do for his Leaving Cert.

He expected her to put it in the bin and go on and on at him about how disappointed she was. He hated having rows with his mum and he kept racking his brains, trying to make up a lie that would defuse the situation before she got into full flight.

His Mum's Story
James was perfectly correct about his mother Anne finding the condom, but she didn't react as he anticipated. She brought it up to his room and left it on his bedside

table. Then she sat down and had a good think about what she would say to James when he got home. He was a lovely, healthy young man of seventeen and she wasn't sure if he had the condom for personal use or for a 'just-in-case' scenario.

She suspected that his girlfriend Sharon was far more sexually experienced than James. Of course, she had never said this to him, but it was at the back of her mind. Mothers know these things. Anne felt relieved to find the condom in James's jeans. At least if he *was* having sex, he was acting responsibly and taking precautions against pregnancy. She had been putting off getting his dad to have a talk with him, but now that she had found the condom, it created a window of opportunity that made it irresponsible to put it off any longer. She hoped her husband would agree to talk to James. She felt she would be too uncomfortable, so either his dad would talk to him or she'd have to let the matter rest.

THE SCANDAL OF IRRESPONSIBLE PARENTS
'The Scandal of Teenage Pregnancy' is a popular newspaper headline that gets widespread media coverage. The even bigger 'scandal', of irresponsible parents who fail to tell sexually active young people that no contraception is 100 per cent safe and expect them to find out for themselves about protection, remains hidden. Teenagers are advised to engage in responsible sexual behaviour by adults who fail to discuss with them how to be sexually responsible. Inadequate sex education is due to lack of communication between parents and children.

Adults are very poor at talking to teenagers about

contraception and protection. They rarely check that young people have accurate information, so the popular myths about birth control remain unchallenged. It's not unusual to have boys claim that contraception is a woman's responsibility, or that condoms interfere with sexual pleasure. Both sexes are reluctant to ask for contraception. That's understandable, because when you are young and inexperienced, getting condoms is like declaring to the world that you intend to have sex.

Some school programmes deal with how to put on a sheath or explain that there are risks involved in what we call 'safe sex practices'. Many others don't.

The condom is the only contraceptive that can significantly reduce the risk of contracting an STD. A fact that is seldom acknowledged is that access to a rubber johnny or condom does not guarantee that it will be used correctly.

Advertisements for 'safe sex' don't give the full picture. They never suggest in any way that condoms can and do fail when they are not used correctly. Before you read on, see if you can list the three things a person needs to check before they open the packet holding the condom.

- If there is any damage to the packet, it's not safe, so throw it away.
- Make sure it has a quality mark and is made by a reputable company.
- Check the use-by date. If it has passed, put the condom in the bin.

In many families, women believe it is the father's job to talk to the boys. Men who can joke freely in the pub about sex and swap raunchy stories are frequently unable to face the challenge of bringing up the subject of protection with sons, even when they suspect they are sexually active and may be at risk of making a girl pregnant. There is a perception that mothers find it easier and some do. I know this sounds unusual, but it's true. In some areas, parents can go to classes to learn how to talk to children about sex and growing up. I hope there is a huge take-up of these classes and that this generation of young people will be the last to have parents who can't talk to their children about sex.

It Won't Happen to Me

Some sexually active young people tend to be very irresponsible when it comes to using protection. They are fully aware of the risks of unplanned pregnancy and how to prevent it, yet fail to use contraception. It's amazing to find otherwise intelligent people who believe that sex should be spontaneous and unplanned and who make a conscious choice not to use contraception. Risk-taking is so much a part of adolescence that it is difficult to warn youngsters that a potential partner could have an STD and put them in danger, and that a brief sexual encounter could affect the rest of their life.

Beliefs like, 'It couldn't happen to me' or 'I'm too young for this to happen' or 'I can't get pregnant the first time' are crazy. I find it astonishing that any sane person can claim to believe that you can't get pregnant the first time you have sex. Of course you can. You can even get pregnant by having intimate genital contact without penetration, which is why all condom packets carry a warning that there should be no genital contact before the condom is put on and after it is removed. It's terrifying that so many teenagers don't know that when a man has an erection, his penis produces a tiny drop of lubricating fluid that contains sperm. If genital contact occurs with his girlfriend and the conditions are right – her body is producing the mucus that keeps sperm alive – pregnancy can occur without penetration.

FACE REALITY – YOUNG PEOPLE HAVING SEX

It is difficult for many parents and sex educators to acknowledge that young people are sexually active. They are reluctant to teach them about contraception or mention STDs in case it encourages them to experiment sexually. This kind of misguided over-protection does more harm than good. I'm tempted to suggest that it should come under the heading of child neglect, only that is too harsh. I have no doubt that the people who confuse innocence and ignorance mean well. They are just out of touch with the reality of life for this generation of young people, who are sexualised from an early age, reach puberty well in advance of their teens, and will have to deal with intense peer pressure to have sex before they leave school.

In every generation, teenagers were always told to save sex for marriage, and in every generation, the majority chose to ignore that advice and engaged in a little thrill seeking. A radical change in recent times has been a huge shift away from the snogging and intimate touching that gently introduced teenagers to sexual activity somewhere around their mid-teens. Today, sexualised adolescents are likely to engage in everything short of intercourse without any awareness of the risks.

Is it any wonder that so many parents believe that you can't stop teenagers having sex? Again, if we are being really honest, we'll admit that some parents accept that young people do have sex at an early age, and warn them to use protection. Others do the best they can to encourage young people to delay having sex until they are in a serious, committed relationship. Few young people feel well informed. I am frightened to meet young sexually active people who claim to use protection and have never heard that condoms can be damaged if they are used carelessly.

One-night stands are not a good idea; they are potentially very dangerous. Yet after any big match or rock-concert family planning clinics expect to be busy dealing with clients who had unprotected sex. An alarming statistic is that for one third of teenagers first sex happens on a one-night stand. The morning-after pill or emergency contraception is widely used by girls who want to avoid an unplanned pregnancy but it offers no protection at all against STDs.

Condoms: Easily Damaged

A condom is also known as a rubber, johnny or frenchie. It's a thin latex (which is like a very fine rubber) sheath that is rolled onto the erect penis before any genital contact takes place. When the man ejaculates, the semen is held in the end of the condom. The man has to withdraw very carefully soon after he has ejaculated or the condom may slip off. The penis becomes limp or flaccid quickly and shrinks back to its normal size.

It is widely accepted that practising 'safe sex' means using protection. Yes, using a condom may protect from an unwanted pregnancy and infection with the HIV virus that causes AIDS. However, the manufacturers warn that no contraception can guarantee 100 per cent protection. Although condoms are very strong, they can still be torn by sharp fingernails, rings or even rough skin. When they are used correctly, they can protect against unplanned pregnancy, some sexually transmitted diseases, cervical cancer and HIV/AIDS. Unfortunately, many people don't use them correctly. They don't follow the instructions and, surprise, surprise, the condom fails.

Oil-based pessaries or lubricants such as petroleum jelly, baby oil, body lotions and massage oils can cause damage that makes a condom ineffective. Let's be real and honest about what is going on in the real world. Sexually active young people believe they are engaging in 'safe sex practices' when in fact they are engaging in high-risk behaviour that can lead to potentially life-changing consequences. A spermicide should be used by the woman for extra safety. She can either insert cream or jelly into her vagina using a special applicator, or insert a pessary with her fingers. This is a small soft tablet that melts inside the vagina.

You need to understand that condoms cannot protect against all sexually transmitted diseases. It is true that high-quality condoms use a spermicidal lubricant which contains Nonoxynol 9, a chemical that not only kills sperm but can also protect against HIV. Unfortunately, they are not effective against other virally transmitted diseases, like genital herpes and genital warts. Condoms sometimes burst. They can also leak when you take them off. People who use them for intercourse often don't use any protection for oral sex, which, while it is less risky, is not totally safe. There is a lot of evidence to suggest that teenagers are having sex earlier and with more partners. They are more willing to have sex than to talk about it and a good deal of the blame for contraceptive failure stems from a failure to communicate. A very simple rule that is really easy to remember is, if you can't talk about it, you're not ready to do it.

CONDOMS ARE NOT 100 PER CENT SAFE

If you depend on a condom and think you are protected and enjoying 'safe sex', think again. You are under an illusion that needs to be shattered. The belief that wearing a condom offers complete protection against STDs gives a false sense of security. The HIV virus is 450 times smaller than a single sperm, so even a naturally occurring defect in the latex of a condom could allow the virus to get through. Be warned. Condoms can and do fail, and the result of condom failure may be either an unplanned pregnancy or infection with HIV or one of the other STDs.

Condoms offer protection only to the part of the body that is covered by the sheath. Diseases like genital warts can be picked up from exposure around the genital area. Genital herpes can also be spread to the areas of the genitals not covered by the condom, including around the anus. The bottom line is that there is no contraceptive protection available that is 100 per cent safe against both pregnancy and diseases.

Failure of Contraception

Twenty-three-year-old Sarah and Colin have had their plans to marry upset because Sarah has just found out that she is probably about five and a half months pregnant. She has been living with Colin for almost three years. They found that using condoms interfered with the spontaneity of their lovemaking, so two years ago, Sarah asked her GP to prescribe the contraceptive pill. After a scare when she forgot to take a pill, she went back to her doctor and asked for the three-month injection. It was great not to have to remember to pop that little pill. Sarah and Colin were able to relax.

Everything seemed to be working fine over the following months. Sarah got her regular injections, and although she was more tired than usual, she put it down to the fuss around the wedding preparations. Colin thought she looked unwell after a stomach upset and suggested she go along to her GP for a check-up. He ran a couple of tests that all came back negative before he suggested that she should have a pregnancy test done. She was pregnant.

The Contraceptive Pill

In the 1960s, the contraceptive pill began to be widely used and for the first time women had control over their own fertility. They were able to enjoy sexual pleasure without much risk of pregnancy. The pill is a very effective method of contraception when used as prescribed. The failure rate is about 3 per cent in women who take it as prescribed and much higher when not taken as directed. The combined pill is slightly more effective then the mini-pill, which contains only progesterone (the combined pill contains oestrogen and progesterone). It has to be prescribed by a doctor and the woman needs regular check-ups to make sure that she is not suffering from any unhealthy side-effects. The pills vary in the way they work.

The Combined Pill

This is taken daily for three weeks out of four. It prevents conception by tricking the body into altering the hormones released by the ovaries so that no eggs ripen in the ovaries and ovulation cannot take place. If an ovum (the Latin word for an egg) is not released, the egg can't be fertilised and pregnancy can't occur. It also causes thickening of the cervical mucus so that the sperm cannot penetrate it, and it alters the lining of the womb to make it less likely to accept a fertilised egg.

When it is not taken as prescribed, pregnancy can occur. Failures occur when a woman forgets to take her pill. Doctors can give an injectable contraceptive which is inserted into the muscle, where it is released slowly, giving protection for up to three months. It contains a similar hormone to the minipill. If there is a problem with side effects, it can't be removed from the body and the woman will have to live with the unpleasantness

The Mini-pill

This has to be prescribed by a doctor and needs to be taken even more carefully then the combined pill. It is taken at the same time every day: if a woman forgets and is three hours late taking it, she is not protected. It doesn't always stop the ovary releasing an egg (ovulation). It works by thickening the mucus at the cervix which makes it difficult for sperm to get through and enter the womb. It has fewer known side effects than the combined pill.

SIDE EFFECTS

There are possible side effects with every type of medication. One good side effect of contraceptive pills is that periods become lighter, more regular, and less uncomfortable. With the mini-pill, some women have no periods at all. Breakthrough bleeding – that is, bleeding at odd times of the month – can occur for a small number of women.

Taking antibiotics for an infection can reduce the effectiveness of the pill, as can weekend episodes of binge-drinking. If a woman is drunk or ill and vomits or has diarrhoea, it can interfere with the working of the pill. She should continue to take it, but may not be protected from the first day of vomiting and for the next seven days. It is recommended that she use another method of contraception for that week.

Girls with irregular periods and women with period problems are often put on the pill. The not so good side effects include weight gain, headaches, nausea, sore breasts, depression and feeling less sexy. Usually these effects lessen after a few months, and if they persist, changing to a different type of pill may help.

Doctors will not prescribe the pill for some women. It's not suitable for women over thirty-five, especially if they smoke. A woman who has diabetes or epilepsy, or who has previously had blood clots, or has coronary disease or breast cancer is usually advised not to take the pill.

The Male Pill

We have been hearing about a pill for men for many years but it appears to be a long way off. Researchers are testing drugs and synthetic hormones but it will be a long time yet before they are tested and given approval.

Other Methods of Contraception

Femidom

The female condom combines features of the male condom and a diaphragm. It is like a long polyurethane bag, closed at one end, with an inner and outer ring. The inner ring is inserted into the vagina and the closed part fits over the cervix. The outer ring rests on the vagina. Aesthetically, it is not very pleasing to look at and it is not widely used. The one advantage it has is that the couple can remain cuddled together for as long as they like after they make love. A disadvantage with the male condom is that he must withdraw after he ejaculates, or the semen may be spilled when his penis becomes flaccid.

The Sponge

The sponge is made of a polyurethane foam sponge which contains a spermicide. Some women may be allergic to the spermicide. It is inserted into the vagina, covering the cervix. It is effective for twenty-four hours. It must remain in place for six hours after sex and be removed within thirty hours. The sponge not widely available, and has a high failure rate.

The Diaphragm or Cervical Cap

The dutch or cervical cap is smaller and fits more tightly over the cervix than the diaphragm. The diaphragm is a thin rubber device shaped like a shallow domed cup, with a rim to allow for insertion, because it needs to be folded to be inserted in the vagina. It can be awkward to insert, because you have to put a spermicidal cream or gel on it before insertion. If a couple get their second wind after intercourse and want to have sex again, additional spermicide must be added. It works by blocking the rear part of the vagina and prevents any sperm getting to the cervix. The couple can't feel it during lovemaking. Women who have weak pelvic muscles can have difficulty holding the diaphragm in place and would be recommended to use the cervical cap. They both work in similar ways.

A woman needs to be measured for a diaphragm by her doctor. She inserts it herself before having intercourse. A small gain or loss of about three kilograms in weight can stop it fitting properly. It must be used with a spermicide. It's not a very popular form of contraception because it has to be placed in the vagina before intercourse and left there for six hours afterwards. After use it is cleaned by washing in warm water, rinsed and dried.

The Coil or Intra-Uterine Device (IUD)

This is a small coil or loop made of plastic and copper which is inserted in the womb by a doctor trained in family planning. It can be kept in place for a few years. The woman will not be aware of it and has to do regular checks to make sure it is still in her womb by looking for a thread which is left hanging down in the vagina. It is not recommended for young women who have not been pregnant.

There is controversy about how the coil works. It either prevents the fertilisation of the ovum or its implantation in the uterine wall. IUDs can cause heavy or painful periods and increase the risk of infection. There is a risk of pelvic inflammatory disease (PID) if a woman with an undiagnosed STD has a coil inserted.

There are two basic types of coil: ones that contain hormones, and ones that contain copper. If you want to use this method of birth control, will need to ask your doctor for advice.

Natural Methods

These methods rely on abstaining from sex during the time of the month when a woman is likely to conceive. In theory, a woman can become pregnant only when she is fertile, around the time of ovulation, so if she avoids intercourse for those few days, she can avoid becoming pregnant. The problem is that it is extremely difficult for a woman to predict ovulation with any accuracy. Many women do not have regular periods, and even those who have a regular cycle sometimes have irregular months. In practice, forget about trying to make any predictions about when a woman can conceive. I have met teenage girls who got pregnant from having sex at the end of a period, early in their cycle and a week or even a few days before the next period. The bottom line is that any time a woman has sex, she can get pregnant. Let me repeat. *Any time a woman has sex she may get pregnant.* Get the message? *No contraception is 100 per cent safe.*

THE SAFE PERIOD

This is very difficult to predict. It is not simply a matter of counting the days in the menstrual cycle, subtracting fourteen from the highest number and saying, 'That's when she ovulates.' This is another of those terrifying myths that many teenagers believe and act on. A GP, Dr Gerry Waters, and I were on a radio programme to discuss teenage pregnancy. He was adamant that he had women patients who had conceived just after a period, just before a period, and at every stage in the middle. He said he didn't care what the textbooks said, he was convinced that conception could occur at any time in the menstrual cycle.

THE TEMPERATURE METHOD

Couples try to work out the safe period from the dates of the woman's periods. Her temperature rises slightly when she ovulates, and to find out when her safe period is, she takes her temperature first thing every morning before she gets out of bed with a very sensitive thermometer. When the egg is released, it will rise slightly – between 0.4 and 0.8 degrees Fahrenheit. If the temperature remains higher for three days in a row – that is, higher than all the previous six days – she will have ovulated. Illness, shock and stress can interfere with temperature readings. If she thinks she has ovulated and refrains from unprotected sex around the time of ovulation, in theory she can't become pregnant.

In practice, the failure rate is high. The egg is believed to live from one to three days. It used to be believed that sperm could live inside the woman's body for five days. Recently scientists have found that they can live there for seven and even up to ten days. If a woman has sex early in her cycle she could have sperm living in her fallopian tubes, ready to rush to the ripened egg and impregnate her as soon as it is released.

Cervical Mucus (The Ovulation or Billings Method)

This method relies on observing mucus. A woman's mucus or bodily discharge alters during her cycles. Immediately after her period, it is thick, sticky and opaque. Then it becomes clearer, wetter and slippier as she becomes more fertile. The clearer and more slippery it is, the more easily sperm can survive in it. On the day of ovulation, it is clear and stretchy, then it changes in texture and returns to being thicker and sticky.

The Sympto-Thermal Method

This is a fancy name for combining the calendar, body temperature and cervical mucus methods. It has a high failure rate. If a woman is over-tired it can cause her temperature to rise. If she has a vaginal infection, the consistency of her vaginal mucus can change.

Withdrawal

When a couple are making love and the man withdraws before he ejaculates, it is called withdrawal, or *coitus interruptus* and it is a most unreliable method of contraception. Don't use it if you want to avoid pregnancy. A woman can become pregnant if her partner ejaculates on the labia or near her vagina. Younger men rarely have the control to recognise when they are about to ejaculate. The probability is that much of the sexual experience of teenage boys is limited to masturbation, which is often done very quickly. Withdrawal frequently leaves the woman feeling dissatisfied with a partner who has relieved himself.

STERILISATION

This is a surgical operation to make either a man or woman permanently incapable of having children.

VASECTOMY

Male sterilisation is an easier procedure than female sterilisation. Under a local anaesthetic, the sperm ducts are cut and tied so that the sperm cannot travel down the penis. The man can still have an erection and ejaculate. Some sperm still remain in the man's body after the operation, and he needs to have a test done on his semen before he can have unprotected sex.

After a vasaectomy, a man's testicles will continue to produce sperm, but they will now be absorbed into the body. Sperm makes up only 0.5 per cent of the volume of the ejaculation so he has no need to worry about his sexual performance. His ejaculation won't look or feel different. If he changes his mind about the vasectomy, surgery is usually not successful in reversing the procedure.

Tubal ligation

A woman who has her tubes tied has to have an operation under a general anaesthetic. It's called a tubal ligation. The most usual method is for the fallopian tubes to be closed by a clip or plastic ring so that the egg cannot pass down to the womb. This stops the egg and sperm meeting. A woman will continue to have her periods and enjoy a normal sex life. It is the most effective method of contraception, but if a woman changes her mind and wants to have a baby, there is no guarantee that the procedure can be reversed. In rare cases – about four in 1,000 – the tubes grow back and a woman can become pregnant. Sterilisation is a permanent way to avoid pregnancy and should only be contemplated by people who have already completed their family.

9

Sexually Transmitted Diseases (STDs)

Ruth and Dan

Ruth and Dan were second-year college students who had been dating for several months. They were madly in love and faithful partners, so when Dan began to have difficulty with painful urination, he assumed that he had picked up some kind of urinary infection. The college doctor thought so too, and prescribed antibiotics, but they didn't really help. Despite repeated treatment, his symptoms persisted. When his scrotum became tender, with a painful swelling on one side, the doctor suggested that he be tested for sexual diseases. Dan was shocked to discover that he had a sexually transmitted infection called chlamydia.

He found it very hard to tell Ruth he had an STD and to ask her to be tested. She went for the test, knowing that she was symptom-free and convinced that she would get a clean bill of health. She didn't. The doctor in the STD clinic told her she carried chlamydia and said she was a very lucky girl. If her boyfriend had not been diagnosed and her disease remained untreated, she could have become infertile.

Ruth was aghast when she discovered that she was responsible for originally infecting Dan and continuing to reinfect him so that the repeated antibiotic treatments failed to clear his infection. They both responded well to treatment and are fine now.

Over Thirty Sexually Transmitted Infections

If you are sexually active, you are at risk of picking up a potentially dangerous and possibly fatal sexual disease. It takes just one exposure to one infected partner to contract an STI. Most people don't know that there are more than thirty different sexually transmitted diseases. You will often find them referred to as sexually transmitted infections (STIs); sexually transmitted diseases (STDs), or the more old-fashioned term, venereal diseases (VDs). It's not unusual to find that a person is infected with more than one. The scary bit is that you can't tell by looking at someone. Not everyone who is infected with an STD has any symptoms, so some people can have a disease without knowing it. This is especially true of women.

A person who does not have symptoms can infect a partner without either of them knowing that there is a problem. It can take months – or up to a year or even more with some STDs – after infection before any symptoms appear. What this means is that an infected person who is sexually intimate with more than one partner can infect others. By the time a disease or diseases are diagnosed, a great number of people may be infected.

Almost everyone knows about HIV, the human immunodeficiency virus which causes Acquired Immuno-Deficiency Syndrome (AIDS). The virus is deadly, yet a person can be infected for many years before they have any symptoms. Once someone is infected, there is no cure and although researchers are working hard they have not succeeded in finding a vaccine to protect against this fatal disease. Most of the other sexually transmitted diseases caused by a virus can be treated but cannot be cured. Those caused by bacteria can be cleared up quite quickly once the correct treatment is prescribed. The problem that prevents early treatment is the lack of symptoms. Until a person discovers they have a disease they won't go for treatment, and for some people by then it's too late.

If left untreated for too long some of these infections can cause sterility. This is why I say that a decision to become sexually active could genuinely be a life or death decision. Be honest with yourself. If you have a potential partner who could infect you with HIV, wouldn't you want them to tell you? Would you then go ahead and have sex? Would you trust a condom to protect you? Suppose you discovered that a partner had genital herpes, an STD that can be treated but not cured, what would you do? Would you take the risk? It's hard to believe that in the heat of passion, people do take the risk. A few moments of pleasure can lead to a lifetime of regret.

If you're a woman, you need to know that infection for you is more serious than for a man. It may cause miscarriage or stillbirth, and some infections, like herpes, can be passed on to newborn babies. Your life and your future sexual health depend on the choices you make.

How Many People Have You Been With?

Here is the really scary bit that not everyone understands. When you have sex, you expose yourself to the germs of every person that you and your partner have been intimate with, and also to the germs of every person who has been intimate with each of those people before you or your partner. Let me spell it out. The first time you are intimate, you could find yourself exposed to germs from the bodies of twenty or thirty or even more people.

You don't have to have intercourse to be at risk. Any intimate touching that involves genital contact is a potential source of infection. Let's suppose Joe and Claire have sex. It's her first time. Joe was intimate with two previous girlfriends. That means Claire has 'been with' three people, plus the partners with whom they have been intimate. Imagine that one of those girls slept with a guy who had three previous partners. Claire is connected with six or more people. Joe was the first guy the other girl had had intercourse with, but she had engaged in oral sex with four different partners. That brings the number Claire has been with up to more than ten. If I continue to trace back to see who was sexually intimate with whom, we could find out that the unfortunate Claire, who is having sex with Joe for the first time, is exposed to the germs of thirty, forty or maybe even more people.

Of course, she didn't physically have sex with every one of those people, but if any one of them was infected or was incubating a disease, she is at risk. Be warned: when you are sexually intimate with a partner, you are exposed to the germs of every person who has ever had intimate sexual contact with that partner.

You Can't Tell by Looking
Like most people, you probably think that you are safe: none of your friends would have such diseases. A great

deal of potentially dangerous information gets passed around peer-educated groups. Some wrong beliefs that are widespread are: clean people don't catch these diseases; you have to be promiscuous to be at risk; the best way to get rid of an STD is to give it away.

It's amazing how sexually active people agree that they know people who might get caught and be a party to a pregnancy, but they are adamant that they don't know anyone who has a sexual disease. That's another of those dangerous beliefs that puts lives at risk A partner who looks perfectly healthy may not be disease-free and could put your health at risk. A person who is infected with an STD may have no symptoms at all, or such mild ones, like a slight fever, that they fail to make the connection.

If you have sex with a partner without knowing their sexual history, you may be at risk. If you intend to make a decision that could possibly have such lifelong repercussions, you had better make sure that you are fully educated about all the long-term consequences of genital sex. If you are under the illusion that practising 'safe sex' will definitely protect you from an unplanned pregnancy and ensure that there is no possibility of contracting STDs, you have only half the picture. You don't know what you are doing. Get the kind of accurate information you need.

COULD YOU BE AT RISK?

Parents expect young people to make good choices about their sexual behaviour when they don't have the full facts. If nobody has explained to you that the consequences of engaging in sex with a partner who is not a virgin can be fatal, you are sexually miseducated. You have been denied vital information and sexual ignorance may be putting your life at risk.

The mistaken belief that doctors can cure all STDs other than HIV also needs to be challenged. While crabs – the slang term for pubic lice – and thrush can be easily cured, others conditions are there for life. If a woman's tubes are blocked because she didn't get early treatment for a disease, that can't be cured.

It's crazy to think that no one you know has an STD, or that you can't be infected the first time you have sex. There are thousands of young men and women who contracted an STD the first time they had sex. Let's be real and admit what we all know. People who are sexually active make risky partners. If you have sex with someone who is not a virgin, you are at risk. If someone who is a virgin has sex with you after you have been intimate with a different partner, even if it was six months or a year ago, you yourself are a potentially risky partner. Some STDs can take up to a year after infection before there is an outbreak of symptoms. During that time, the person may be totally unaware that they have contracted an infection or could be passing it on to a sexual partner or partners.

What Diseases Are There?

Here is a list of some of the more common diseases: chlamydia; genital herpes; genital warts; gonorrhea; hepatitis B; HIV; pelvic inflammatory disease (PID); pubic lice; syphilis; thrush; trichomoniasis; vaginitis.

Almost everyone knows the consequences of contracting the HIV virus. Other STDs caused by viruses are not life-threatening, but they certainly are quality-of-life changing. Living with outbreaks of a painful virus that weaken your body with flu-like symptoms, and putting up with discomfort in the genital area is no fun.

Medical concerns include the longer term risks of infertility, cancer and AIDS. These are risks that people don't talk about openly, so sexually active people seldom consider that there are potentially serious consequences to having sex when you or your partner is not a virgin.

CHLAMYDIA

This is one of the most worrying of the STDs because it is a major cause of infection in men and women. It is a common factor in pelvic inflammatory disease (PID), which can lead to infertility and an increased risk of an ectopic pregnancy in women. Since the late 1980s, it is the most common STD in both North America and Europe.

It is difficult to identify. Only one in three women with chlamydia have any symptoms. It can be successfully treated by antibiotics. If it's not diagnosed and treated, it can cause scarring of the fallopian tubes, sterility and chronic pelvic pain. In men, the first symptoms are usually painful urination or pus coming from the penis. Chlamydia is thought to be responsible for about half of all infections of the epididymis, which can cause tenderness in the scrotum and painful swelling on only one side. It can be transferred with the hands from the genitals to the eyes.

The symptoms when they occur are similar to many other STDs and include burning sensations and increased frequency of urination and discharge from the penis or vagina. It is not unusual for these symptoms to disappear without treatment. Because it's often accompanied by gonorrhea, the two are usually treated together.

GENITAL HERPES

This is another incurable STD that is caused by the herpes simplex virus, similar to the common cold sore. The most usual symptoms are a rash with a cluster of white, blistery sores. The rash and small painful sores can cause pain, itching or burning sensations around the vagina, cervix, penis, mouth, anus and other parts of the body. Other symptoms can be swollen glands, fever, headache and flu-like symptoms. The first outbreak can be very severe. Attacks range in severity from mild to debilitating.

The sores take an average of fifteen to twenty-three days to heal. Pain gradually gets worse over the first week and reaches its peak between seven and eleven days. It's really distressing when active, and although recurrent infections are likely, their duration is generally briefer. About half those who have genital herpes have five recurrences or more a year, with men having slightly more than women. From the time the tingling sensations that precede the infection are felt until the sores have healed fully, there should be no genital contact. Symptoms can vary in severity from one outbreak to another.

Herpes cannot be contracted from clothing or toilet seats, but studies show that that some people can spread the disease even when they have no sores. Condoms protect only the part that is covered. During sex, bodily secretions can leak over the pelvic area and you need to be aware that condoms don't offer full protection. If the sores are active during childbirth, the baby will have to be delivered by Caesarean section.

Cold sores on the lips are caused by the herpes simplex virus and can be transmitted by kissing or drinking from the same cup as a sufferer. Your local doctor can give you a leaflet that will explain how to avoid spreading the virus to other parts of your body. There is no specific cure. A number of remedies ease pain and ward off further infections.

GENITAL WARTS

These are one of the most common STDs. They are small non-cancerous fleshy growths on the skin of the genitals that feel hard and gritty. They are usually felt before they are seen. They are caused by the human papilloma virus (HPV). You don't have to have genital sex or oral sex to pick up genital warts. Close genital to genital contact can cause infection. Occasionally people who engage in oral sex can get genital warts in their mouths, throats and lips. The warts that people get on their hands are unlikely to be transmitted to the genitals because they are caused by a different type of virus.

It can take anything from two weeks to a year or more for genital warts to appear on the body but it normally takes about three months. A person may be infected with HPV and never have visible warts, though they may infect someone else who could then develop warts. There is strong evidence to link genital warts and cancer of the cervix. A woman who is infected must have an annual smear test.

GONORRHEA

Sexual intercourse is the main source of this infection, which is also known as 'the clap'. It's caused by bacteria and it's estimated that as many as 80 per cent of infected women and 10 per cent of men will have no symptoms, so many who are infected simply don't know. It is spread through genital and oral sex. Untreated gonorrhea can cause sterility, arthritis, heart problems and disorders of the central nervous system. In women it can cause PID, which can lead to ectopic pregnancy as well as infertility. When diagnosed, it can be cured quickly with antibiotics. Early detection and treatment is essential to avoid sterility. It is frequently accompanied by chlamydia and the two are treated together.

For those who have symptoms, a slight green or yellow-green discharge from the vagina is common within about ten days. This will be accompanied by frequent and often burning urination. Pelvic pain, tenderness in the vulva and other flu-like symptoms can occur. For those who come late for treatment, the consequences can be infertility and lifelong pelvic pain. In men, it usually causes a painful discharge and discomfort on urination. Homosexual transmission is very common.

Hepatitis B

This is the only STD for which there is a preventive vaccine. It is even more contagious than the HIV virus and can be transmitted through intimate physical contact and through sexual contact. Kissing, drinking from the same cup or sharing needles can infect a person.

Hepatitis B is common among intravenous drug abusers and can cause severe liver damage and death. This is another of the viruses that has no symptoms during its most contagious phases. No medical treatment exists. Sufferers can be made comfortable with a healthy diet and rest but they can't be cured.

There are two stages. One to six months after contact, flu-like symptoms, tiredness and pain in the joints occur.

Stage two includes jaundice, brown urine and soreness in the abdominal area.

HIV

The reason everyone knows about HIV is that it is a deadly disease. It is most commonly passed on through sex with an infected partner or by sharing needles. It is not widely known that women run a higher risk of becoming infected from one act of intercourse than men. A mother who is HIV-positive can pass the virus on to her unborn baby and contaminated blood products have also passed on the disease. A person can be infected for ten years or more and not show any symptoms. During that time, the virus will be weakening the body's ability to fight infections. There is no vaccine but there are some drugs that can help to prolong the life of a patient and delay the onset of AIDS.

Pelvic Inflammatory Disease

PID is not really an STD but a bacterial infection. When a genital infection in a woman has spread into her reproductive system – the womb and fallopian tubes and the ovaries – we say she has PID. It may be a consequence of untreated gonorrhea or chlamydia. Whether treated or not, it can lead to sterility, ectopic pregnancy and chronic pain. Treatment usually includes antibiotics and bed rest. Surgery may be required to remove abscesses and scar tissue or to repair or remove damaged reproductive organs.

The symptoms include fever, nausea, chills, pelvic pain, spotting and pain between periods or urination, heavy bleeding with blood clots during periods, unusually long or painful periods and pain during intercourse. The more often PID strikes a woman, the higher her risks of being infertile.

Pubic Lice

These are popularly known as crabs because they resemble tiny crabs when viewed under a microscope. They feed on human blood and are primarily spread by sexual contact, although they can be picked up from contact with infected bedding, clothing and toilet seats. Their bites cause intense itching which leads to scratching, redness and skin irritation. Pubic lice like hairy places and can be found in the armpits, beard and eyelashes. On close inspection, the lice and their eggs can be seen by the naked eye. Non-prescription medications are available from a pharmacist or drugstore.

Syphilis

Syphilis is caused by bacteria and can be cured with antibiotics. There are three stages of infection. The symptoms begin with a sore on or in the vagina or on the man's penis. The sores can appear on the genital area within one to twelve weeks after infection. These may disappear, and two to six months later, new symptoms may occur. A rash around the genitals, sore throat, mild fever and sore glands may develop with other, flu-like symptoms. These will also disappear. The final stage, which can be up to thirty years later, includes damage to the heart, brain and vital organs. Unless treated, syphilis will last a lifetime, and a person who unknowingly contracts the disease as a teenager can pass it on to a spouse or an unborn child. Unlike gonorrhea, syphilis spreads throughout the whole body shortly after it enters.

Thrush

Thrush or *candida albicans* is caused by a fungus and is readily treated by cream administered to the affected parts or pessaries – soft tablets which are inserted directly into the vagina. The symptoms are an itchy, white vaginal discharge, irritation of the vulva, inflammation of the penis or testicles and a kind of yeasty smell. It's not usually spread as an STD, but it can be, and it's more likely to be transmitted by oral sex than by intercourse.

Trichomoniasis

This produces an itchy, smelly discharge and is treatable with special tablets. It is caused by a small parasite. Men frequently don't get symptoms. Women get a frothy vaginal discharge that causes itching and a burning sensation during urination. Some women get symptoms only during or immediately after their periods. The partner needs to be treated to prevent reinfection. Trichomoniasis is responsible for about a quarter of cases of vaginitis in women and is one of the organisms that can cause nongonococcal urethritis (NGU) in men. This is the term used to describe any inflammation of the urethra not caused by gonorrhea.

Vaginitis

If you have any burning or itching in the vaginal area or any discharge or unpleasant odour you are probably suffering from vaginitis. It can be triggered by several different organisms and is spread through sexual contact. Men carry the organism but since many don't have symptoms, both partners must be treated to prevent the infections passing back and forth. Treatment varies with the cause of the disease.

What Can You Do to Protect Yourself?

The only way to be 100 per cent safe is to remain a virgin and delay having sex until you meet another virgin who has never intravenously abused drugs. If you enter into a monogamous, mutually exclusive relationship, that means you and your partner have sex only with each other, you are at no risk of catching an STD. Be aware that virginity is often claimed by people who have not had intercourse but who have engaged in genital touching, mutual masturbation and oral sex – all risky behaviours.

Learning about so many potentially serious diseases is enough to make anyone paranoid about safer sex and that may not be such a bad thing. If it makes people afraid to have one-night stands, and encourages them to think about the importance of waiting to have sex until they get to know their partner well and can talk about life, love and sexual history, I won't complain.

Women are more likely to catch diseases from men than men are from women, and let me repeat, they can be infected even when they have only been intimate once. If you have been sexually active and engaged in any risky behaviour, even if you have no symptoms, go and have a medical examination if you are worried. Ask to be tested for the common, often asymptomatic STDs. At best, you will be sexually healthy and free of disease. If you have caught a disease, at least it will be diagnosed early and treatment can begin.

10

Straight Talking About Coming Out

Mark's Story

For as long as he can remember, Mark has been fascinated by naked men. One of his earliest memories goes back to when he was about four years of age. He has a vivid memory of going into a locker room with his father and being fascinated by the men in the showers. His father was the captain of a rugby team, so he had access to the men's shower area.

His mother was ambitious for her two sons to succeed. She had mapped out their lives for them, from careers to marriage, and was even specific about the gender of grandchildren she wanted. By the age of sixteen, Mark knew he was gay, and went through a few very difficult years. He felt trapped, unable to be himself and afraid to relate to other people in case anyone found out. When he was asked any personal questions, his muddled perception of homosexuality and his hatred of it made him freeze inside.

During his early teens, Mark's parents were delighted that he didn't pay nearly as much attention to girls as his brother. His mother always claimed that girls took his brother's mind off his studies, and he would be better off putting his energies into preparing for a good career. However, by the time he reached his late teens and went away to college, they were genuinely concerned that he had never had a girlfriend.

His father encouraged him to socialise, and once he even suggested he should talk to someone about being so moody. 'It's not healthy to be such a loner,' he complained. Only his grandmother, who lived with them, suspected what the problem might be. Mark was very close to her, and one evening, they happened to be watching television together. The programme was about homosexuality. It was a turning point for Mark.

His grandmother applauded the courage of the gay men in the audience who spoke up for themselves. She commented on how surprised she was that they looked so normal. 'They're different from us and they have a right to be accepted,' she said.

'I'm different too,' Mark blurted out. His grandmother reached over and put her hand on his hand, giving it a little squeeze. 'Wouldn't it be a dull world if we were all the same?' she said, as she smiled at him with love and acceptance in her eyes.

Mark had always feared that if anyone knew he was gay they would reject him, that his life would be ruined. Coming out to his grandmother gave him the confidence to go to a meeting of a gay and lesbian group. For the first time, he was free to express himself socially. He realised that he couldn't continue to isolate himself as he had done before.

When Mark found a boyfriend, he was transformed. His

parents were curious about the very obvious changes in him. They were delighted that he was so happy and becoming more outgoing. He was reluctant to tell them that he was gay because he was terrified that his family would put him on trial and ask him to defend a lifestyle he had barely experienced. They didn't.

On Christmas morning, his parents came back from Church and were very friendly to his friend, Des. Then Mark's mother winked at him and asked him, 'Why don't you invite your partner to stay to lunch?' Mark almost collapsed with shock. It was so unexpected. He had guessed his brother knew, but they had never discussed it. He couldn't believe that his parents also knew that he was gay and would accept him for who he was.

What I find so sad about this happy tale is that Mark's fears about rejection came from the wrong assumptions he made about how other people would respond to his homosexuality. The poor guy went through years of unnecessary misery. He put himself through torture thinking that his family would reject him when his problem was that he couldn't fully accept himself.

WHAT IS SEXUAL ORIENTATION?

Sexual orientation is the label people put on themselves to describe whether they are heterosexual or homosexual. Homosexuality is defined as a predominant and persistent preference for sexual arousal by persons of the same sex and a weak or absent arousal by the opposite sex. In Greek, hetero means different and homo means the same. Heterosexual people are men and women who are sexually attracted to the opposite sex. The majority of people are heterosexual. A minority are homosexual. Homosexual men like to be called gay and homosexual women like to be referred to as lesbian or, less commonly, gay.

I would love to be able to give you accurate figures for sexual orientation among the population at large, but I don't have that information. For example, a book for children called *Understanding the Facts of Life* published by Usborne claims that one man in ten is gay. The Kinsey Institute *New Report on Sex* suggests that it is necessary to define what you mean by 'homosexual' before the question can be answered. Some people claim to be heterosexual yet live a gay lifestyle. They said only about 4 per cent of men were exclusively homosexual throughout their entire lives and 2–3 per cent of women were exclusively lesbian throughout their entire lives. The gay and lesbian community believes that the figures are between 4 and 10 per cent.

Much confusion about sexual orientation is caused because people do not know that it is perfectly normal to experience strong feelings for a person of the same sex, especially during early puberty. This is a normal part of adolescence and is not the same as true homosexuality. It's important to remember that sexual feelings aroused by a person of the same sex, fantasising about having a same-sex partner or even engaging in sexual activity with a same-sex partner are not accurate predictors of one's adult sexual orientation. There is evidence to suggest that one man in three has had at least one same-sex experience. Yet nobody would be tempted to suggest that one in three men has a gay orientation.

UNCOVERING YOUR SEXUAL ORIENTATION

Adolescence is not an easy time for any boy or girl. For a young person who thinks that he or she may be gay, it is made a lot more difficult. From early adolescence, a boy who doesn't fit the stereotype or popular image of masculinity is at risk of being labelled 'gay'. Girls are rarely labelled lesbian in early adolescence. One reason for this is that there is a widespread understanding that, early in puberty, girls get crushes on other girls. Boys who feel an attraction for a classmate or a teacher or sports star of their own sex feel they have to keep this hidden. If they openly acknowledge how they feel, they will immediately be labelled.

In our homophobic culture, many young people are terrified of this label and the insulting and demeaning names that go with it. This is a bigger problem for males than it is for females. Any schoolboy who doesn't fit the accepted masculine image is vulnerable and at risk. Of course there are fashions in what is and is not considered acceptable. For anyone who is not wearing the right gear and hairstyle the teasing can be incredibly cruel and very damaging to self-confidence. To protect themselves, some boys who feel they are not heterosexual force themselves to conform. They date girls to avoid the hassle and prejudice.

There is a great deal of controversy about when and how young people discover their sexual orientation. In our culture it would be very rare to find a teenager who has never worried about whether they are gay or straight. Most gay and lesbian adolescents feel different. They know they are not straight. Few are comfortable about discussing this with their parents so they live with feeling different and unsure. Many struggle alone with the uncertainty and confusion this brings. They have strong feelings that they don't quite fit in with their peers, but how do they find out whether this is part of the normal adolescent process or if it means they are gay?

It can be very helpful for anyone in this situation to look up the telephone numbers of gay helplines. The volunteers who run these lines will be able to put you in touch with discussion groups for people who have had no contact with other gay people. You may be pleasantly surprised to discover how many different support groups are organised by the gay community for gay people and their parents.

We live in a heterosexual society, so to whom can the teenager or young adult who thinks he or she may be gay turn for advice? She or he is unlikely to have any real-life role models to look to or to ask, 'How would I know if I'm gay?' The truth is that all of us come in contact with gay people every day of our lives. They are among our family and friends, teachers and work colleagues and we don't know it because there is so much prejudice in our society that they conceal their orientation.

It's hardly surprising then that most young homosexual people are afraid to discuss their orientation. They fear telling their parents and this is understandable, particularly while they are financially dependent on them. Horror stories about parents who threw gay adolescents out of the house with nowhere to go are not always to be believed. In a tiny number of cases, intolerant parents have shown that kind of rejection, but happily this extreme reaction is becoming rare.

It makes good sense to talk to other gay people who will have a better understanding than someone who has not been through this struggle. Older gay people can usually date their first suspicions about their sexual orientation to primary school. Many had an awareness from puberty, or sometimes even earlier, of having a predilection for erotic fantasies about same-sex friends and finding themselves totally unmoved when their peers were falling madly in love, besotted by the opposite sex in early puberty. Late heterosexual developers whose hormones are slower to kick in may worry that they are not as sexually charged as many of their peers who seem to have sex on the brain and hormones on the verge of eruption.

Identifying sexual orientation needs to be based on more than feeling sexy when you read about gay sex or even having fantasies about same-sex activity. Close relationships are often formed between young teenage boys and experimental sex play often goes along with this. This may take the form of masturbating together or actually masturbating each other. I have heard stories about boys having competitions about who can ejaculate the farthest. Usually, this kind of activity doesn't go any farther. This sort of sexual behaviour is fairly common and does not indicate gay tendencies. It would be foolish to believe that teenagers who mess about in that way are gay. Some may very well be and others are simply going through a process of experimentation. Some boys who are in boarding school fool around, have a same-sex relationship and then go on to be predominantly heterosexual. It is equally true that many homosexual people experiment with relationships with the opposite sex and go on to be gay.

If you are gay or lesbian, that is only one small part of your personality – who you are. Yet if you come out, be prepared for mixed reactions. If you are incredibly lucky, you will meet with nothing but acceptance. That is the best possible scenario and it is rare. More usually, there will be some family and friends who will allow this one part of you to define who you are. It may take time for parents and other family members to recognise the courage and strength of character it takes to 'come out' and acknowledge you are gay. (To 'come out' means to tell people you are homosexual.)

Why Do Parents Get Upset?

Gay and lesbian teenagers are reluctant to 'come out' because they are afraid of how their parents may react, and not without good reason. There is widespread ignorance and a lot of prejudice that feed the myths, like those that suggest gay people have no sexual boundaries, that they are utterly promiscuous and go around seducing young innocents. So it's understandable that learning that a teenage son or daughter is gay is usually a bit of a shock, but not always.

Occasionally one or both parents suspect and there is relief all around that something that everyone knew and nobody talked about is now out in the open. Families are different, and there is no way to predict how a parent may react to the news that a son is gay or a daughter is a lesbian. It has to be admitted that some parents react very negatively, but that, in time, most come around. Even when a parent has had some suspicions, it nearly always comes as a shock when a young person comes out. When a parent responds negatively, they are reacting to feelings of disappointment, ignorance, and fear.

Most parents have dreams for their children. There is a common expectation that young adults will get established in a career and in time settle down with a partner, get married and have children. Can you understand that when a parent discovers that their dream scenario is not going to happen, they have mixed emotions? Naturally there is disappointment. They need time to grieve about the wedding that will never be celebrated, about the grandchildren they are not going to have, and if we are thinking about an only son, about the family name dying out. Don't minimise how important all these considerations are.

Then there is the old chestnut that rears its head in almost every family, whether the problem is a teen pregnancy or a gay child: 'What will the neighbours think when they find out?' 'What will we tell other family members?' 'Is this inherited? We never had anything like this on our side of the family!' Add to this the fears bred by the popular beliefs about the gay lifestyle. Don't underestimate how scary it is for a parent who has read about the promiscuous behaviour, multiple partners and rampant AIDS among the gay community and believes it to be true. When you take all of these factors into account, you have some idea of the trauma that hits parents when they find they have a child who is homosexual.

If gay couples were free to be more open about their monogamous relationships, it might not be so frightening or difficult for a parent to accept the truth. It takes time to come to terms when any perceived crisis hits a family. Some parents feel that having a gay child reflects badly on them. They blame themselves and think they must have done something wrong. Most ask questions that cannot really be answered. 'What caused this?' 'If he or she was reared differently, could this orientation have been avoided?' 'If only I had done this or that or the other thing, this might never have happened.'

Some parents of gay people are in denial. They assume homosexuality is just a phase that the person will grow out of when they get married and have children. Because of the taboos in society and religious beliefs, they find it too difficult to accept that they have a gay or lesbian family member, and deal with it by denying that it is permanent. If they pray enough or protest enough, they hope that in time it will go away. They need to learn that it doesn't.

For decades, scientists have tried to discover what causes homosexuality, without success. Studies have been done with both identical and fraternal twins, but the findings remain inconclusive. There are theories about gay genes and about differences in brain sizes, but no proof. It has been suggested that a certain part of a gay man's brain is the same size as a heterosexual woman's, and smaller than the same area in a heterosexual man's brain.

The pressure that society puts on gay people forces many to live a lie and hide or deny their orientation. This is an heavy burden for any person to bear. Psychologists say that suppressing thoughts and feelings can lead to severe depression and other psychological disturbances and illnesses. Studies show that the rate of suicides for young homosexual men is much higher than for heterosexuals of the same age. One reason put forward for this is that many gay men are unable to cope when faced by rejection from their families. Parents need help and support to deal sensitively with a gay teenager. Check the front of the telephone directory for the names and telephone numbers of support groups for gay people and their families.

IGNORANCE BREEDS PREJUDICE

There is probably more ignorance and prejudice about homosexuality than about any other sexual issue, including STDs. Many people believe that homosexual people choose their sexual orientation, that one day they wake up and make a conscious decision to be gay. It's easy to understand why people who think like this believe that all a gay person has to do to become heterosexual is to have a change of mind and switch back.

Until relatively recently, homosexuality was regarded as a mental illness in some societies, and many gay men were put into institutions to be cured of their deviant behaviour. It is horrific to think of the terrible way some of these men were treated by doctors who administered shock treatment, gave them drugs and incarcerated them in an effort to make them conform and become 'normal'.

Aversion therapy was also given to cure gay people and change their orientation. The theory was that aversion therapy worked by encouraging the patient to respond physically and feel sexual pleasure in response to homosexual fantasies. At the height of pleasure, they would be given an unpleasant electric shock to condition the body against such reactions.

Over the centuries, there have been all sorts of explanations for what caused people to be homosexual. Sigmund Freud believed that homosexuality developed when a boy identified with his mother rather than with his father, and that lesbians were possessed by love for their mothers. Other psychological theories claim that lesbians identify too much with their fathers. Freud said the heterosexual woman is a female who has successfully negotiated her initial bond of love and identification for her mother.

There is a widespread misconception that childhood sexual trauma or abuse can turn a person into a homosexual. This is clearly not the case. Many people who are gay were never interfered with as children and many people who were molested as children are not gay. Gay men and women come from a wide range of family backgrounds.

Despite the fact that research shows that most paedophiles are heterosexual men, there is a widespread myth that homosexuals molest children. Of course, some gay men and women have abused children, but child sexual abuse is not sexually driven. It's about power and violence. In most cases, the abuser is a family member: a father, uncle or brother. However, we are now also finding men who were abused by women coming forward.

Another common myth is that gay men dress up in women's clothes. It is not well known that transvestites – men who wear women's clothes for pleasure – are nearly always heterosexual. When gay men dress up in women's clothes, it's called drag. It's the kind of over-the-top behaviour that is meant as a deliberate parody and is very different to transvestism. It's never done for sexual pleasure.

It Says in the Bible

Traditional church teaching and attitudes to homosexuality are beginning to soften as psychological insights give more understanding of sexual differences. Different denominations have different interpretations of Bible teaching and both Christians and Jews use the story of Sodom and Gomorrah to condemn the sin of homosexuality. Today, many theologians say that the story has been misinterpreted. The passage that is most frequently quoted to denounce gay men is Genesis 19, 4-11:

> But before they lay down, the men of the city, the men of Sodom, both young and old, all the people to the last man surrounded the house; and they called to Lot, 'Where are the men who came to you tonight? Bring them out to us so that we may know them.' Lot went out of the door to the men, shut the door after him, and said, 'I beg you, my brothers, do not act so wickedly. Look, I have two daughters who have not known a man; let me bring them out to you, and do to them as you please; only do nothing to these men for they have come under the shelter of my roof.'

The modern interpretation is that the people were punished for their lack of hospitality, not because of their homosexuality. Isn't it odd that there is no condemnation of Lot's behaviour? He was prepared to send out his virgin daughters to the men, to do with as they pleased. Yet I have never heard this quotation used as an argument to suggest that the Bible does not value virginity.

In the Book of Ezekiel 16, 49-50 we are told that the sin of Sodom was not male homosexual lust.

> This was the guilt of your sister Sodom: she and her daughters had pride, excess of food and prosperous ease, but did not aid the poor and needy.

Texts in both the Old and New Testaments which refer to homosexuality are being carefully studied. The passage in the New Testament, Romans 1, 26-27 is often quoted.

> For this reason, God gave them up to degrading passions. Their women exchanged natural intercourse for unnatural and in the same way also the men giving up natural intercourse with women were consumed with passion for one another. Men committed shameless acts with men and received in their own persons the due penalty for their error.

Modern theologians argue that what is condemned is the idolatry of the Gentiles who were worshipping false gods. In Biblical times, fertility cults and all sorts of sexual practices were part of idol-worship practices.

Lesser-known passages like 1 Samuel 18, 1-5, which suggest a more positive understanding of same-sex relationships, are overlooked.

> When David had finished speaking to Saul, the soul of Jonathan was bound to the soul of David, and Jonathan loved him as his own soul. Saul took him that day and would not let him return to his father's house. Then Jonathan made a covenant with David, because he loved him as his own soul. Jonathan stripped himself of the robe that he was wearing, and gave it to David and his armour; and even his sword and his bow and belt.

Dominican theologian Donald Goergen says, 'Any theology of homosexuality must include a discussion of relationships such as the above. There are different ways of being homosexual and different ways of being heterosexual. Christian understanding praises relationships seen in the context of love, fidelity, permanence and living in Christ through the Spirit.'

It is rather surprising that Jesus did not teach about homosexuality. He taught about love and self-acceptance. The two great commandments he gave us are: 'First you shall love the Lord your God with all your heart, with all your soul and with all your mind. And the second is like the first, you shall love your neighbour as yourself. On these two commandments depend all the law and the prophets.'

Some Christians and Jews condemn homosexual people as sinners. They fail to separate the person from the action. I am convinced that people who cite scripture to condemn others 'know not what they do'.

Religious people who condemn gay men and lesbian

women are probably unaware that their behaviour is unloving or bigoted. Some people are deeply hurt by this lack of tolerance; others are not. Many gay people are deeply spiritual and have a strong faith. The Lesbian and Gay Christian movement supports them and offers understanding to those who feel unwelcome in their own church.

Many of us miss this truth. Whether we are aware of it or not, we love our neighbours as ourselves. The way we treat others mirrors how we treat ourselves. I cannot give to others what I do not have for myself. If I am harsh and judgemental with myself, that is how I will treat you. If I don't know how to love and accept myself, how can I love or accept you? If I am compassionate with myself, I know how to be gentle and understanding with you. When you understand this, it makes it a little easier to forgive people who show prejudice or who judge you and put you down. If they see you as a sinner or as failing to measure up, it tells you a lot about how they see themselves. They need your compassion, not your judgement.

STAYING IN THE CLOSET

Some people hide their gayness for their whole lives. We say that they are 'in the closet'. The vast majority of gay men look, act and speak just like heterosexual men. The number who look effeminate, mince around with a limp wrist, wear outrageous clothes or speak in a falsetto voice is tiny. The same can be said of the majority of lesbian women. Only a very tiny minority look, act and speak in a butch way. Some young men and women are so fearful of admitting that they are gay that they compare themselves to the effeminate or dyke stereotype and think that because they don't speak or act like that, they must be straight.

Life is very difficult for a person who tries to deny as integral a part of themselves as their sexuality. Yet some men and women who are in denial will adopt a heterosexual lifestyle in order to hide the truth even from themselves. They may marry and have children and regularly have sex with their spouse. Some may even display homophobic attitudes to cover up their inclinations. Yet at the same time, in order to get excited, they have to fantasise about having sex with a member of their own sex. This is a real tragedy. They live in fear of ever being truly themselves, because of the danger of being found out. They tell themselves that they couldn't survive telling their secret. Despite the anti-discrimination laws that give legal protection to gay people, there is a great deal of ambiguity in people's reactions when a person comes out.

You can understand why some gay people spend their life in the closet. Some cope by hiding their sexual orientation and avoiding close or intimate same-sex relationships. This makes for a very lonely way of being in the world. The pressure gay people feel in a society that is prejudiced causes untold damage to health and relationships. An awful lot of people get hurt when either heterosexual or gay people adopt a lifestyle to which they are not suited when eventually the truth comes out. It cannot be denied that some married men find release in gay bars. It's not difficult to imagine the kind of pain that is caused when a gay person who is married to a heterosexual partner and has children gets found out.

The AIDS crisis has brought into the open the clandestine lifestyle of many people who appear to be heterosexual but live gay sex lives. We have already seen that people tend to lie about their sex lives. There can be a difference between how a person labels his or her sexual orientation and their actual sexual behaviour. Research shows that between 62 and 79 per cent of men who label themselves homosexual have had sex with women. Kinsey found that around half of college-educated women had at least one same-sex erotic experience past puberty.

Coming Out

Coming out is a life-changing decision that should never be taken lightly. It can be a very scary experience to come out for the first time because there is a real risk of rejection. It is difficult for any teenager to confront their newly emerging sexuality. It is a lot more complex for a gay person who has no way of knowing how family and friends will react to the revelation that he is gay or she is lesbian.

If you believe you are gay, having second and even third thoughts about coming out to the person you have just met and find incredibly sexy is necessary. What if he or she turns out to be straight? What if it's even worse, and not only are you rejected, but the person is repelled by your sexual advances and calls you a pervert? There is less of a risk of making a mistake in a gay club or pub.

Unfortunately, poor sex education, which always comes from poor communication with parents, leaves young gay people vulnerable, without adequate information to decide whether to come out of or stay in the closet. In most families, there is an unspoken fear of homosexuality. Boys are discouraged from playing with dolls and dressing up in case it encourages them to become gay and cross-dress when they are older. Our society is more accepting of physical demonstrativeness between women. Nobody raises an eyebrow when girls come into school in the morning and greet each other with a hug. If guys behaved in the same way they would be jeered at and mocked. This is not because teenage boys are not affectionate, it's simply because they are more likely to be labelled gay than girls.

There are also very wide differences between what is seen as acceptable behaviour in different situation. It's acceptable for males to jump on top of each other and embrace every player in sight when they score a goal on the playing field. Yet if one of those same guys hugged a mate when fully dressed, to congratulate him for scoring a goal during another match when he played well, he would be judged totally differently. Behaviour that is acceptable in the heat of the moment in a match is regarded differently barely an hour later.

It's much the same with gay bars and night clubs. Two men or two women holding hands in a gay bar wouldn't get a second glance. In a straight bar, the same behaviour may be considered so unacceptable that the couple may be asked to leave.

When a gay person comes out and it is a positive experience, it feels like a huge burden has been lifted from their shoulders, because they no longer have to pretend and live a lie. They are free to live the way they want without fear of who may see them and talk.

Most universities and colleges have gay and lesbian societies. Many of the people who attend events they organise are straight, so if someone is not sure and just wants to check out the scene and meet some gay people, they can do so without coming out. Of course, there is a possibility of meeting someone who is out to pick up a partner. Isn't that what many students set out to do when they socialise?

It wouldn't be fair to ignore the fact that for some people, coming out is a very negative and painful experience. As a result of admitting they are gay, they feel rejected and ostracised by some family members. That is a very heavy price to pay for admitting the truth. Many people who come out to their families choose to be extremely careful about who they tell at work, as openness about sexual orientation may not enhance their career prospects.

If you have read this far, you know that I am a strong believer in open and honest communication. The truth sets us free and a truth that you must never lose sight of is that you bear no responsibility for hurting anyone who is upset by the news when you come out. Their feelings come from their own response and from how they think. Only you can decide whether the advantages of living openly as a gay person outweigh the risks you take in coming out. It takes courage to make that decision and perhaps the wisest advice is to test the water by coming out to friends first. Good luck!

11

Finding Your Dream Partner

Maria's Story

From her early teens, Maria had dreamed about being in love. The partner she imagined changed all the time. She pictured herself with pop stars and rugby players, local boys and older men. Her dream locations changed too. Sometimes she met her dream man in a secluded wood, other times beside a beautiful lake or in a posh restaurant. Occasionally she even created the fantasy in the privacy of her home. The characters and scenery changed, but the feelings in her daydream stayed the same.

It always began the same way. The man walks up to her, smiling. Her face lights up and she delights in the way he really sees her. His eyes caress her face adoringly and she feels so secure. His hand brushes her cheek and her whole body tingles at his touch. 'Hi Maria,' he says softly. 'I missed you.' He reaches out tenderly and draws her to him. He kisses her lovingly and she thrills to his touch.

Her arms go around him and she returns his kiss gently. She enjoys the closeness, the intimacy of their meeting. There is no pressure to do or be anything other than she is. When he looks at her, she feels that he is really seeing her, that he has very deep insights into who she is. She is filled with warmth in his embrace, and he is so happy to enjoy that intimate time with her.

Her dream partner always makes her feel cared for and unconditionally accepted. In some fantasies, he says something that makes her giggle or surprises her so that she laughs with delight.

Unfortunately, when she comes out of her fantasy life and returns to reality, her experiences are very different. The men she meets are never like her dream partners who know how to make her feel loved. The guys she meets in real life are not that interested in what she wants. The bottom line is Maria wants to feel valued and loved while the men she meets seem to be more interested in sex without commitment.

Check Your Beliefs

When you fall in love, do you want it to last for a few weeks, or months, or are you interested in having a long-term committed monogamous relationship that will lead to marriage? The way your parents relate will have a huge influence on whether you see a long-term future for yourself with the person you choose.

Do you have a belief that there is only one Mr or Ms Right for you? That belief will limit your choices. Do you believe that there is only one perfect partner out there who will make you happy? If you do, I suggest you have a rethink. If you want someone else to make you happy, you are setting out to have a dependent relationship and that's not a good idea. Do you believe in fate? If you choose to wait to see what destiny has in store for you, fine. Better still, discover that you have a major part to play in creating your own destiny.

Your experience of love for you is affected by what you believe. When you are open to new experiences and believe there are many potential partners in the world that could be the one for you, you will meet lots of people to whom you relate really well. Do you have beliefs about who chooses whom? Will you actively seek out the person you want to spend your life with, or do you have an expectation that they will come knocking at your door to look for you? All your beliefs will influence the kind of dream partner you think will make you happy. They also determine what love means to you. As you mature, you will find your beliefs change, and as they do, the image you have of the dream partner you want in your life will change too.

When you fall in love, it's quite usual to find that your picture of your ideal partner changes. You suddenly find that the characteristics of the person you are with go to the top of the list of qualities your dream date should have. If you want a serious relationship, I would encourage you to question every belief you have about the kind of person you think will make you happy. It's a myth that if you love each other, everything will work out right in the end. It won't just happen.

Relationships take work and perseverance and understanding of where you are both coming from if they are to grow. If none of your relationships up to now have worked, it's time to stop complaining that you are just unlucky. The truth is that you are making poor choices because you have wrong beliefs. Only you can find out why you make those choices. If you stay in a relationship with a person who treats you badly there is no doubt that you lack self-esteem. If you don't feel good about yourself, you will suffer from a lack of self-confidence, and one result is that you will let people mistreat you. Poor self-esteem makes it difficult for a person to demand respect. Always speak up for what *you* want.

Begin this instant to become aware that you have choices about self-esteem. Listen for the negative messages you give yourself or that you accept from others and reframe them. Stop saying things like: 'I'm hopeless at cooking, sports, maths' – whatever. The message you give yourself is: 'This is how it was in the beginning, is now and ever shall be.' Change it to a more positive message that offers the choice of change, and say: 'I'm not good at it, *yet*.' By reframing like this, you stop putting yourself down and acknowledge that you *can* get good at the task if you choose to put in the work and develop the skill. When you feel you have no choice, you are disempowered; you feel controlled from outside. When you realise that in every situation in life you have choices, what a change you will see.

What Do You Want From a Relationship?

Be honest. Do you know what *you* really want from a relationship? You may say you want to feel loved, adored and cherished and if you were asked to explain what a partner would need to do for you to have those feelings, the chances are high that you wouldn't know. They are lovely words and impossible to put into effect. We don't have the language to describe our feelings accurately. Can you love someone when you focus on how you want *them* to make *you* feel? Is it wise to give away that power? Too often, what people wish for and think would make them happy is so emotionally unhealthy that it can only lead to misery. You might well as, why anyone would set himself up to be miserable? Well, no one does it deliberately, but people unconsciously create situations that give them the feelings with which they are familiar.

If you read the chapter on parents, you will know that so often, when you think you are freely making a choice, you're not. It's the mother or father in your head that's deciding you need a solid, sensible boyfriend who will hold down a good job, or a warm-hearted kind girl who will cook and make a nice home. If you are still in the rebellious stage where you set out to do the opposite to what your parents want – and some people never leave it – you may hang around with a handsome guy who refuses to work because he wants to be a pop star, or date the sexy girl who flaunts her breasts because her ambition is to be a topless model. If you are unconsciously choosing partners of whom your parents would disapprove, how can your relationships have any chance of long-term success?

The less life experience you have, the more vulnerable you are to making poor choices. At sixteen, your friends have more of an influence on the choices you make than when you are twenty-six. Say you're a sixteen-year-old girl and the nineteen-year-old boy with whom you're in love tells you he really cares about you. Of course you want to believe him when he says 'I love you'. Those words can get the logical part of your brain to switch off. You'll ignore the friends that warn you about how fickle he is. You won't care that they say he never stays in a relationship or that he has a reputation for dumping girls once he's had sex with them. When you are in love, you will block all that is negative out. Like thousands before you, you'll fall into the trap of believing that this time it will be different because he chose you. At twenty-six you are more likely to listen because experience has taught you life lessons. Do you know that the best predictor of whether or not a relationship will last is the opinion of friends, not the couple's judgement?

THE RIGHT CHEMISTRY

You can do nothing to make someone fall in love with you or to stop them falling out of love. You could find someone who fits your shopping list for a dream partner, and if the chemistry isn't right it won't work. When you hear people say love is blind, believe them. It doesn't matter whether you are nine or ninety, when you fall in love, your brain chemistry changes.

People in love are hooked on a love drug. Scientists tell us that our brain produces a range of chemicals when we fall in love that make us feel intoxicated. The newer the experience, the more chemicals are produced and the more potent the effect. The bad news is that the high doesn't last, and within as little as eighteen months, the most potent love chemical, phenylethylamine (PEA), can no longer produce the same reaction. As with any drug, the longer you take it, the more of it you need to get the buzz.

Oxytocin is often referred to as the snuggle-up or bonding chemical because it builds the desire for closeness. It is believed that this is the drug that is responsible for the urge to hug and be held by your partner. When a woman has sex, her brain produces oxytocin, and one of the effects of the drug is that she feels emotionally involved with a man. If you are a reader of the problem pages in women's magazines you will frequently come across queries from women who feel they have an irrational attachment to a man with whom they had a one-night stand, or who went into a relationship with the agreement that it was to be a 'no-strings-attached' one and now, in spite of themselves, they are emotionally involved. Blame the drug.

Couples who have sex before they have a relationship are rarely aware of these love drugs that the body produces naturally. That's why, when people say a couple are blinded by love or intoxicated by love, they are right. That is why all of us have the experience of hearing a friend talk about this wonderful person they are dating and when we finally get to meet the date we can't see what is so special. The person seems so ordinary that we find ourselves wondering what she or he sees in him or her, as the case may be. You may even have had the experience of falling madly in love with someone at one time in your life and, when you meet them later, you are puzzled. You have no idea what you saw in them or why you found them so attractive. You were blinded by the love drug.

Love Is Blind

We blind ourselves to reality when we are in love. There is a chemical cause for why the brain gets scrambled when someone is in love. Almost every woman who is looking for her dream partner wants the chemistry to be right. She wants that special something that makes her thrill to the sight of her loved one, that has her heart beating faster at the sound of his voice. Men are more likely to want a good-looking woman with a great body that thrills them with a sexy excitement. A man desires a woman who visually turns him on.

Looks are more important than feelings for men. Women desire a man who makes them feel beautiful and interesting and fascinating. Both sexes want that sense of being connected and in tune, of feeling really understood, and in the early stages of being in love, they can have it all. This is a recognised part of the idealised awareness that happens during the initial stage of the euphoria that people who are in love experience.

Whether you are sixteen or twenty-six or forty, it's only natural that your body will respond sexually when you are in love. You will enjoy sexy dreams. I always tell students that it's exciting to find a partner who has the power to make your senses feel intoxicated, and I'm delighted to confirm that falling in love does make people literally drunk with joy even if a drop of alcohol never crosses their lips. The bliss of finding a soulmate who seems to sense what you're thinking and feeling gives a certain sparkle, a way of being that is unmistakable to anyone who is watching.

People who are in love come alive in a way that is obvious even to complete strangers. Their eyes are brighter, they have a different energy, they look radiant and intoxicated because that is exactly what they are. The high of being in love is chemically induced by PEA but its effects are not permanent. It is estimated that it lasts for about eighteen months in adults, and although I haven't seen any studies to confirm this, I suspect that it is there for a much shorter period with younger people. Could it be that the average sixteen-year-old's romance only lasts about forty-five days because the PEA runs out?

Feeling Intoxicated

Love involves a certain chemistry that takes most people by surprise. So when you fall in love, savour every moment. Scribble their name, draw little hearts with arrows through them, look up their star sign and find out what the omens are for your love life. Pick the petals off a flower to see if 's/he love me, s/he loves me not'. Bore your friends silly telling them all about this wonderful being that you can't stop thinking about. Throw their name casually into every conversation. Let your imagination run riot and picture the two of you together two years down the road, five years down the road, twenty years on. Enjoy seeing them smiling and laughing with you in your daydreams and in your dreams at night too.

Enjoy this glorious intoxicated state when everything is perfect. In that early stage, love blinds each partner so they can't see any flaws in the beloved. Falling in love is all about how good the other makes you feel. The hormones go into overdrive, the body tingles with desire. What is so fascinating about this is that the euphoria, and the highs it brings can happen even when those feelings are not reciprocated.

When you get it – when you understand that your

feelings come from how you think, from inside yourself, you will have learned a powerful life lesson. This means *your* happiness does not depend on finding the partner of your dreams. It depends on what you think and what you choose to believe.

When you fall in love, everything feels so wonderful and so different from what you have experienced before that it's understandable that you think your beloved makes you feel that way. She or he doesn't. The beloved stimulates feelings that are in you, but cannot create them. No one outside of you has the power to make you feel anything, because your feelings are the response your body makes to your thinking.

Give me a chance to explain. When a twelve-year-old girl comes rushing into school on a Monday morning throbbing with excitement because she is in love, her feelings of being in love are very real to her. Her eyes sparkle, she looks radiant, she's obviously excited by this pop star for whom she has fallen and probably may never meet. Where do all those powerful feelings that change her physical appearance come from – the pop star or herself? You're right, they come from her thinking, created inside her head – from what she tells herself.

When you fall in love, what creates all those amazing feelings in you is your own thinking. When you understand this, it makes it easier to understand why people fall out of love. They have a change of mind. You may have expected me to suggest that they have a change of heart, but that is not as accurate. Love and sex have far more to do with your brain than with your body. They have more to do with what you think than what you do.

Many new-age teachers say that we create what we believe in, that when you believe something is true, it becomes true for you.

LOVE AT FIRST SIGHT

Researchers say that love at first sight happens in only about 5 per cent of relationships. Men and women fall in and out of love in different ways. It will be no surprise to learn that women who fall in love quickly fall out of love equally fast. Men who fall in love usually stay in love longer, and there is a very simple explanation. Guys are first attracted by physical appearance. They fall in love with what a woman looks like, and since it takes time for appearances to change significantly, their feelings don't change quickly.

A woman falls in love with the kind of person she thinks he is. When he turns out not to be as witty or considerate or charming as she had thought, she falls out of love, and the feelings of euphoria that the drug PEA produced disappear. However, if she has had sex with him, the oxytocin that her brain produces will make her feel emotionally involved.

This is one reason why I regularly disagree with students who tell me they believe that it's OK to have sex when you are in love. I don't believe that being in love is a good enough reason to have sex. Let's be real. You can find ten-year-old girls who have all the physical characteristics of being in love and no one in their right mind would suggest that it's OK for them to have sex. Readiness for intimacy has nothing to do with age and everything to do with the beliefs you hold about relationships. Studies show that it is very common to regret having sex too early. You can't turn back the clock: you can't replace your virginity once it's gone.

If you have sex too soon, you may confuse sexual intimacy with affectionate love and that is a big, big mistake to make. If someone loves you, as opposed to being in love with you, they won't leave you because you ask them to delay having sex. If they are in lust with you, they will look elsewhere to have their needs met. You will be better off without a partner who would use you to relieve themselves sexually.

Dream Illusions

Everything is wonderful when people first fall in love – then reality begins to creep in. The dream illusions are shattered as the intoxicated state wears off. Just as there are no guarantees when you fall in love that the relationship will last, so there are no guarantees when you find a partner you love that the love will last for ever.

They say the fastest way to become a martyr is to live with a saint. You may think you want the perfect person, but be warned. You are setting yourself up to be disappointed if you have unrealistic expectations. At twenty, your dream man may be tall, dark and handsome, or your ideal woman may look like a supermodel. At thirty, they will be beginning to age – the good looks will start to fade. At twenty, you may believe that money will make you happy. At thirty, you know it won't.

Do you know why so few people meet their dream partner? I can tell you, but I don't think you will like what you hear. They miss out on meeting the mate they want because they have a wrong understanding of love and no concept of how to communicate the unconditional acceptance that makes another person feel special. Can you understand that a man who is only interested in meeting a size ten blonde women is limiting his options? He is like someone wandering around with blinkers on. He could be surrounded by women who have all the personality traits and integrity he wants, but how can he see them? He is not interested in the person; all he wants is the right packaging.

One of the quickest ways for a couple to fall out of love is to discover that they have different understandings of what it means to be in love. It feels very exciting to be madly in love, but if both people want different things from the relationship, it simply won't work. If you can't talk about what you want and expect from each other, love will die. Honest communication is the lifeblood of any relationship, and if you don't have that, you have nothing.

Self-Delusion

Is it real if it feels like love at first sight? Say Jack and Jill's eyes meet across a crowded room, the chemistry is mind-blowing and before the evening is over, they say 'I love you'. They could both be telling the truth. One could be lying with the intention to deceive. They could both think they were telling the truth and be lying to themselves.

Say Jill has been given a notice to quit her apartment and in three weeks' time will be without a home. She meets Jack and the chemistry is right. Then she learns that he has a lovely two-bedroom apartment in an ideal location near her college. Can you understand how in that situation she could suddenly find Jack so incredibly attractive that she would want to move in with him? How would Jack know if it's really love or if she is manipulating the situation? Or let's take another scenario. Jack wants sex and he believes the only way he can persuade Jill to go to bed with him is to say, 'I love you'. How can she know if he means it or is lying to her? It is possible that he could be lying to himself and have no conscious awareness that he is being dishonest with her.

Every one of us is fine-tuned to pick up the signals that confirm what we want to be true. Anyone who has even one grey cell in their brain knows that people lie to get sex. It is not so widely recognised that people can lie and not be aware they are fibbing. They can tell lies to others without recognising that they are also dishonest with themselves. I can put fancy words on it and say that when anyone distorts, conceals or denies the truth, they are dishonest, or I can put it simply and say that people lie, and if they do, they are not to be trusted.

You would think that the meaning of 'I love you' is self-evident, but it's not. What those three words mean depends on whether you are in an honest or exploitative relationship. One way to find out whether a partner can be trusted is to check out what kind of relationships they have with family and friends. We can't get away from family influences. Self-esteem and character are built in the home so it's important to know if his or her family shares the same values, standards and problems as your family. Frequently the similarities are staggering.

In families where people regularly break promises,

little or big, trust breaks down. They may have good intentions but broken promises breed insecurity and damage trust. If a parent has an affair or affairs, trust breaks down big time. Children tend to carry unresolved issues around trust into their adult relationships. Barbara De Angelis, America's relationships guru, says, 'Character is all important. Personality is the icing on the cake. Character is the cake itself. Don't ask yourself, "Do I love this person and will they love me?" Ask, "Are they capable of loving me the way I want?"'

There is an old song that says 'You always hurt the one you love, the one you shouldn't hurt at all'. When you hear 'I love you', your partner may be telling the truth or lying. When a person tells a lie of any colour, their actions show that they cannot be trusted. You may think that a little white lie is no harm. The truth is that it doesn't matter what colour the lie is if you are found to be untrustworthy.

TRUST ISSUES

We have all met people who claim to have enjoyed an idyllic childhood. They say they felt loved and cherished and never had a moment of unhappiness. I'm not suggesting they set out to lie to us. They are not dishonest people; they are out of touch with reality. We know that what they are saying is not true because there is no such thing as a perfect childhood. They are unconsciously telling lies as a defence mechanism against a painful truth that they are not willing to recognise or acknowledge. For whatever reason, they are not ready to acknowledge how they were emotionally hurt in childhood.

It's wonderful if you have the maturity to be honest about the emotional baggage you bring into a relationship even if you are not yet ready to do anything to heal the past. If you hide it from yourself, you will feel out of touch because you will be living an illusion that is bound to shatter. If you are not ready to look honestly at what you want and for what purpose you want it, that's fine, once you are making an aware choice. If you desire a fantasy relationship that makes you feel adored and cherished, go ahead, enjoy the experience. It's OK to delight in it as long as you are aware that it can't last like that: it will either change or end.

Self-Awareness

Self-awareness is never easy. To be aware takes both work and commitment. The really difficult part of becoming aware is that it is so hard to let go of the illusions you build up around yourself. It's hard to go below the surface, to spiral downwards to find the sacred self that is underneath, to get to the truth.

If you want a life partner who is honest with you, start work on being honest with yourself. It's difficult to acknowledge that almost everyone lies to help them survive. To see how this works in practice, let's go back to Jill who fell in love with Jack at first sight and needed a place to stay. She may have interpreted what was going on inside her in a less than honest way in order to make it OK for Jack to invite her to move in. She couldn't be truthful with herself and say she was using Jack because that would involve guilt. Say she had a belief that it was selfish to manipulate people to get what you want. Rather then admit to herself that this was what she was doing, she made it easier by telling herself she was in love. Then she felt OK about moving in.

Similarly, if Jack says 'I love you' to get sex, he may not just be lying to Jill: he may also be lying to himself. Suppose he has religious beliefs that teach him that it is morally wrong to separate love from sex. It is really difficult for him to acknowledge that he is filled with lustful desires. He can't bear to feel guilty or bad about meeting his sexual needs. It's too unpleasant and so he unconsciously lies to himself. When he changes his thinking and substitutes love for lust, he gives himself permission to have sex.

Fibs change how people feel. Don't be surprised to discover that the dream partner who lies doesn't appear so desirable any more. I'm not so stupid that I fail to be aware of the widespread acceptance there is in our society of white lies, social lies, little porkies, whatever. If because of childhood experiences I learned to lie either to myself or to others to stay out of trouble or to get what I wanted, I have learned to repress the truth.

Isn't it obvious that when people tell lies often enough, they forget they are lying? Some people get so used to lying that they do it without even knowing. This is often the reason why we get the feeling that a person is insincere. Here is another fact of life that you don't get in sex education classes. People who are not aware of the lies they tell are out of touch, living dishonestly, and are most unlikely to be taking care of their spiritual selves.

What Does 'I Love You' Mean?

So often when people say 'I love you' they don't mean that at all. What they really mean is 'You have something that I want so badly I am prepared to lie to myself to get it'. When I lie, I am creating a fantasy. Please understand that many lies are defence mechanisms that allow people to cope. When I am fantasising and dishonest with myself, I am creating an illusion that meets some need I have. As soon as I become aware of what I am really seeking then I can make better choices that are healthy for me.

Cherish your fantasies; they will give you very valuable insights into what it is you really want and for what purpose. Behind everything I want or desire is a perceived need and when I explore deeply, when I do some soul-searching, I always find that at the core of my being I want to feel loved and accepted exactly as I am. Let's just look at some of the very common needs that young people list and discover what soul-searching reveals. Behind every want I have is a need I desire to have fulfilled.

I want to feel intimate and physically close. Why do I want to feel intimate and physically close? Because I want to feel loved. 'I love you and want to move in with you' meets an obvious need for a home and also a need for shelter. Why or for what purpose would I agree to you moving in? So that you will think well of me. For what purpose do I want you to think well of me? So that I can think well of myself. For what purpose do I want to think well of myself? So that I can learn to accept myself. The phrase 'for what purpose' challenges you to go deeper, so keep asking it after every answer and you will come to know your spiritual self – what *you* really want.

You will discover how you are affected by peer pressure when you do this. For example, at twelve everyone else has a boyfriend or girlfriend, at twenty a partner, at thirty a spouse, so I want one too. For what purpose? To meet the need I have to feel accepted and part of the group. For what purpose do I want to feel accepted and part of the group? So that I can feel OK about myself.

Underneath that desire to be loved and accepted by others is the desire to love and accept myself.

I want to feel that someone loves me to meet my need for affectionate intimacy. For what purpose do I want to feel affection? So that I will feel loved.

'I want to sleep with you' could meet my need for rest, affection, intimacy; it might give me a status, to be envied by my friends, or a feeling that affirms my sexual identity. As I keep spiralling down, asking the same question, 'For what purpose do I want this', I will keep coming back to the same answer. At my very core I want to feel loved and accepted.

'I want you to buy me gifts and lavish money on me' meets my need to feel that I am special and valued. Expensive gifts are the outward signs of this. For what purpose do I need to feel special and valued? So that I can feel you love and value me. For what purpose do I want you to love and value me? So that I will come to love and value myself.

What has all this got to do with meeting your dream partner? Very little, really, but my intention is to help you understand that what you believe you want and desire may not be your idea at all. They may belong to your family or to the agony aunt in the magazines you read or come from a romantic video or book. The way to find out where they are coming from is to make a list of your beliefs and desires and ask yourself, 'for what purpose', again and again. Listen to what you tell yourself, and when you put yourself down, ask, 'Why am I saying this?', 'Where did that come from', or 'For what purpose do I say or want that?' This is a deeply spiritual exercise.

GIVE LOVE TO FIND LOVE

I think that as you do this you will decide that there is no dream partner in the whole world who will make you happy. None! You can stop looking because you are the one who is responsible for creating the feelings you choose to have. After reading this book, you hardly need me to tell you that. If you are looking outside yourself to fulfil your emotional needs, if you want someone else to make you happy, what you are seeking is a dependent relationship. You want to make someone else responsible for your happiness, so they press one button and tell you, 'I love you' and you feel wonderful, and they press another and say, 'You look like you're putting on weight' and you're devastated. When you give someone the power to make you happy or sad, you disempower yourself. In the measure that you give away your power, you invite them to control and manipulate you.

If you desire to have a healthy relationship with an equal partner, don't be surprised if you have to struggle with many of the control issues about dominant and passive behaviours that come up in unhealthy relationships. As you deal with them, you will heal many of the emotional and spiritual hurts that you brought into the relationship.

It's said that we have to give love to find love. I always find it frustrating to read things like, 'You should begin by giving yourself the love and acceptance you need' because I don't know what it means. How are you supposed to do it? It is literally as simple as listening to what you say about yourself and, as soon as you hear a negative judgement or a put-down statement, you change it and make it positive. That is how you build the kind of positive self-image that nurtures good self-esteem. When you love and accept yourself exactly as you are, you will draw people to you who will do the same.

Guru Phil McGraw says we teach people how to treat us, and nowhere is this more evident than in our love relationship. When I love and respect myself, you can see it in my body language. You sense when I feel good about myself and when I am pretending. I meet students all the time who are unaware that they have distorted ideas about love and intimacy.

Some tell me that they have their dream relationships with no strings attached. They use sex, alcohol and socialising to avoid intimacy. I am strongly opposed to casual sex, for obvious reasons. People who engage in casual sex are afraid of intimate relationships. I can understand why they tell me their behaviour is normal. It is – for people with their attitudes and values. However, they have to agree that it is physically risky. Emotionally, casual partners are not valued, and it's hardly surprising that when I suggest we look at what casual sex does spiritually, people don't want to go there.

I also meet people who tell me they are desperate to find love and crave an intimate relationship with anyone half-decent. They don't want casual encounters and tell me they can't find anyone with a good personality who wants a committed relationship. Their world seems to be full of people who are only interested in recreational sex with no strings attached. They say there are lots of potential partners if you are interested in bed-hopping and one-night stands, but if you want a committed relationship, the potential partners disappear, never to be seen again.

I suggest that they, too, look at what intimacy means for them, and usually when they go through the soul-searching, they find that they are creating situations to protect themselves. They are telling themselves they want what one is supposed to want – what their peers or family say they should have – and that is not their choice at all. So they unconsciously set up the situations that prevent them getting what they really didn't want in the first place.

All of us know only too well that many people believe they have found their dream partner and he or she doesn't bring them the fulfilment they expected. When a person has clarity about what they want and actively seek it, they usually find it. A dream partner is simply a fantasy, and fantasies are wonderful, to be enjoyed when you are aware you are enjoying an illusion. When you want a serious life relationship, the time has come to drop the illusions about the dream partner, to wake up to reality. When you are in touch with reality, you will see yourself and others in a different way and you will learn that the secret of love comes from within.

12

Your Sacred Self

CARMEL'S LIFE LESSON

There is a very simple exercise that I learnt from Richard McHugh SJ, the author of the neuro-linguistic programming manual, *Mind with a Heart*. It illustrates clearly how important it is to think positively about oneself. The theory is that when a person thinks a negative thought, the flow of energy in the body is disrupted. This can be clearly illustrated by a simple exercise. Find a partner to work with you. Get the person to stand in front of you and extend one arm sideways, parallel to the ground. Tell them to resist as you gently try to push the arm down. Push down gently on the bone of the wrist nearest the base of the little finger, to test their reaction.

After the person's reaction has been tested, ask them to put their arm down by their side, close their eyes, and repeat silently 'I'm a bad girl (or boy).' After about a minute, while the person is still repeating the negative sentence, lift the arm parallel with the floor. Allow your partner to open her eyes and invite her to resist while you press downwards. In almost every instance the arm moves down easily, and for some people, it collapses.

Ask the partner to relax their arm, close their eyes, and this time, repeat 'I'm a good girl' for about a minute. While she continues to repeat the positive statement, you raise the arm, again invite them to open their eyes and resist, and again try to push the arm down, using a light touch on the wrist bone. Usually, it's impossible to budge the arm.

When people think in a negative way, they are disempowered. When they reframe, which means changing to a more positive way of thinking, there is a free flow of energy and they are empowered. Here is the part that I find fascinating. The empowerment occurs even if the statement is not true *yet*. For example, if I say, 'I'm useless at maths', this negative statement disempowers me and puts me in an arm-down position. It's as if I am telling myself that this is how it was in the beginning, is now and ever shall be. When I change it to a positive statement and say, 'I'm not good at maths yet', I'm open to the possibility that I have a choice. If I want to do extra study or to return to college, I can get good at the subject.

The body never lies, and every thought you think is reflected in some way in your body. Our body language reveals so much that we are not conscious of revealing. Intuitively people read body language and pick up how we feel about ourselves. My body mirrors how I think and feel about myself. When I love, respect and accept myself exactly as I am, I enjoy good self-esteem, and that is reflected in my body language. When I think negatively about myself, my body language mirrors that absence of self-love and respect as clearly as if I were to go around wearing a notice saying, 'Treat me badly, use me; it's what

I expect.' My feelings and life expectations come from how I think. I can choose whether I think in a positive or negative way. When I make the holistic choice to recognise and honour my own sacredness, it affects my whole self: body, mind and spirit.

Your Sacred Self

I'm sure all of us have met people who remain in unhealthy relationships because they think they are in love. It's as if they believe that love excuses all sorts of unacceptable behaviour and demands unquestioning loyalty. There is so much distorted thinking about what it means to love someone that when anyone talks to me about love, I ask, 'What does that mean?' I prefer to talk about positive acceptance rather than about love.

By now it must be obvious that I believe that sex for the vast majority of young people tends to be more the 'wham, bam, thank you ma'am' variety than a passionate, erotic encounter that creates deep loving connections. In other chapters, I have gone into many of the external reasons why this is so. They are important and have an impact, but the basic issue that is crucial to how you deal with any relationship is internal: how you accept yourself.

You will have good self-esteem if your family or the people with whom you lived when young respected you and gave you a feeling of being worthwhile. Were they happy to let you be yourself, or did they try to mould you into the person they wanted you to be? If, like most of us, you were given negative messages that made you feel you were not good enough, didn't try hard enough or were a disappointment to parents or teachers, you got the message that you were not OK. People were not happy with you, so you learned to internalise the feeling that there was something wrong with you. What is wrong is not you, but the unrealistic expectations people have of you.

The child who grows up with parents who delight in him or her and give the gift of unconditional love, learns that he or she is loved for who he or she is. The child who is allowed to be himself or herself knows that he or she is special. They find it natural to recognise and honour their own sacredness. Unhappy children who are under pressure to fulfil the expectations of others carry with them a sense of unworthiness. They feel they are not good enough. They grow up with a huge need for approval and are disempowered by their need to please.

Most of us are familiar with the idea of a sexual awakening: the time in a person's life when his or her sexuality wakes up and come to life with full force. We are not so aware that a spiritual awakening is also part of the process of becoming a mature person. Personality growth gives rise to a spiritual awakening which can be experienced in many different ways. For some it emerges gradually; for others it is a conversion experience, and for others still, spirituality is denied or repressed because the person is not yet ready or willing to deal with it.

Philosopher Teilhard de Chardin writes:

> The goal of both the sexual life and spiritual life is union of the individual with God and with others. Sexuality and spirituality are not exclusive of each other and it is only by

integrating the sexual and the spiritual that we fully develop the tremendous capacity to love ourselves, others and God. A repression of any capacity within us can diminish the capacity to love so if I ignore or deny the spiritual part of myself I am cutting myself off from love.'

After a spiritual awakening, a person is more aware of him or herself as a spiritual person within a particular religious tradition, with spiritual needs. For some people, a spiritual awakening involves rejecting their childhood image of God and Church teachings they can no longer accept. For most people, it brings an energy into their lives that opens them up to be better people: to live better, be more loving and more integrated. Often the catalyst for opening up spiritually is the experience of being accepted and feeling loved by a partner.

Theologian Peter van Breemen SJ says one of the deepest needs of the human heart is to feel appreciated and valued. He doesn't say loved because there are as many varieties of love as there are species of flowers. 'For some people, love is passionate; for others, it is something romantic; for others, love is something merely sexual.'

Great sex involves the whole person. It doesn't depend on knowing how to have sex, or being really knowledgeable about positions and techniques; it depends on honest communication between two self-aware people who care deeply about themselves and about each other. The body doesn't lie, and despite what you may have heard about the additional excitement added to sex by engaging in behaviour that is forbidden, a person whose sexual behaviour does not match their beliefs and values can never be fully relaxed. If there is even the slightest hint of hypocritical conflict within, it is expressed in the body.

SELF-ACCEPTANCE

Earlier I suggested that you ask yourself if the person with whom you are in love is capable of loving you the way you want to be loved. It's a good question, but one you can't answer until you first ask how you love and accept yourself. Self-acceptance means you have the freedom to be yourself, that you recognise that there are areas where you need to grow and make changes, and that you are gentle with yourself and avoid doing violence to yourself by forcing growth.

So often a sense of our own sacredness lies dormant until it is drawn out by the warmth of another's acceptance. You are born with many gifts and talents and some may not be recognised by you. Others you may deny, and need encouragement to use. The loving encouragement of another frees something in you that allows you to become yourself. True self-acceptance doesn't lock you in to your past or deny that you make mistakes. It allows you to learn from them, outgrow them and move on with your life.

This may sound like a contradiction. It is only when I feel accepted by someone else that I become free to be myself. When another sees me as special and values me, only then can I truly become who I am. Families tend to appreciate us for what we can achieve. When we are recognised for what we do, we are not special. Someone else can do the same – maybe even do it better. When I feel accepted for who I am then I have the love that allows me to feel free to be truly myself. Only then can I truly recognise and celebrate my own sacred self. Then I can recognise and respond to the sacredness of others.

A very wise priest I know is fond of saying, 'Where there is love, there is God'. Anthony de Mello, that great spiritual master of the twentieth century said:

> God is the very ground of my being, the Self of my self, and I cannot go deep into my self without coming in touch with Him. The awareness of self is also a means for developing awareness of the other. It is only inasmuch as I am attuned to my own feelings that I am able to be aware of the feelings of others. It is only inasmuch as I am aware of my reactions to others that I am able to go out to them in love, without doing them any harm. When I become sensitively aware of my self I also develop a refined awareness of my brother and sister.

Self-acceptance is the secret to discovering if your partner is capable of loving you the way you deserve. An easy way to establish how accepting you are of yourself is to listen to what you say to others. If you are kind and grateful and appreciate the efforts people make then that is how you will be with yourself. Many of the modern gurus tell us that we see others not as they are but as we are. So how you treat others gives you a good indication of how you treat yourself. As you grow in acceptance of your sacred self, you become more accepting, compassionate and creative.

Spiritual people are kind and nurturing to themselves and others. It feels good to be in their company because they have the gift of affirming others and helping them to feel valued. What they do so well is to treat people with reverence. They mirror your own sacredness back to you.

Sex and Sin

The erosion of religious influence is blamed for the radically changed attitudes that people today have towards sex and sexuality. Having the means to control fertility has had an enormous impact on how people behave. Before contraception was readily available, the fear of pregnancy ruled people's behaviour because an unmarried mother was held in contempt and accused of bringing disgrace to her family. Having sex before marriage was a mortal sin that damned a soul. Single parenthood is so taken for granted today that it is difficult for young people to imagine the huge social stigma that used to be attached to publicly falling from grace with an unmarried pregnancy.

Your beliefs involve the whole person, including what you believe about the physical, emotional and spiritual aspects of life and love. You relate as a sexual person. Your moral values are interwoven with your beliefs about right and wrong: how you see your relationships, how you give and receive love and what you hope for and expect from yourself and others.

If you believe that your sexual feelings and desires are natural, you are well on the way to celebrating who you are as a sexual person. If, on the other hand, you have learned to think of sex in a negative way and associate sex and sin, you will have a very different attitude. One of those old noxious weeds that still infects people's thinking is that it is a sin to take pleasure in sex.

Bad religious teaching that tries to impose repressive attitudes to sexual pleasure makes people learn about sex in psychologically and spiritually unhealthy ways. When I work with students, we always discuss the spirituality of sexuality. In my book *Relationships and Sexuality* I explore how the Bible celebrates erotic love and how the intimate relationship between lovers is used by both Jews and Christians to symbolise the relationship between God and his people. Good religious teaching is focused on love. It is psychologically sound.

I always tell students that their relationships are as good as their communication. To communicate well it is more important to be able to listen than to speak. To listen well you need to hear more than the words; the most important part is the heart listening – tuning in to your own and the other person's feelings.

Today we explain sin as a failure to show love. I feel really sad that the archaic language that the churches use to condemn sexual sin obscures a really important message that everyone would benefit from hearing. Young people are greatly in need of encouragement to delay inappropriate sexual activity. Good religious teaching should give them the support they need. Sadly, it frequently doesn't. The churches have a message about the sacredness of sex and sexuality that our world needs to hear. It needs to be given in language that doesn't offend or turn people off.

Religion is not opposed to sex. It is opposed to sex as it is misused. The sin is not in having sex, it is in the failure to show love. Teaching that sex should be saved for a loving relationship like marriage has a lot going for it. It doesn't require a great deal of intelligence to know that if a couple have sex too early in the relationship, the love drugs are activated and if they break up the hurt is deeper. Waiting gives you an opportunity to let the trust in your relationship grow.

Students regularly argue with me that no one nowadays is prepared to wait around for sex. After a few weeks or a few months, if a person is not getting sex, they will leave. This begs a most important question. Is it love if your partner makes demands on you, or is it lust? If someone really cares about you, will they put pressure on you to have sex when you don't want to be intimate yet? If you give in to that pressure, are you acting out of love or out of the fear of losing the relationship? Sex is a vitally important part of a loving relationship. Without friendship and communication, there is no love. Where sex is what the couple have in common, relationships rarely last.

Good religious teaching helps people to recognise and value their own sacredness and that of their partner. As Saint Paul says, 'Love is patient; love is kind; love is not envious or boastful or arrogant or rude; it does not insist on its own way; it is not irritable or resentful; it does not rejoice in wrongdoing but rejoices in the truth. It bears all things, believes all things, hopes all things, endures all things. Love never ends'. (1 Cor. 13; 4-8)

Turn Yourself On

The belief is widespread that stimulation comes from what the other person says or does: that your partner has the power to turn you on or off sexually. Would it surprise you to hear that he or she doesn't? Your body may feel like it is being physically aroused by a partner. However, that stimulation comes from the brain, from how you think and interpret what is happening. So if you feel sexy, you are thinking in a way that creates those feelings in you.

When you physically enjoy sexual intimacy, where do the sensations you're enjoying come from – your partner or your own body? Most people are surprised to learn that their response comes more from their brain than their body. What you feel physically and emotionally comes from what you think and how you interpret what you are thinking.

When someone touches you intimately, you are aware of a physical feeling and your response to those physical sensations comes from how you interpret the action. Suppose Bob and Lisa are kissing passionately. He unhooks her bra and fondles her breasts. Whether it is a pleasant or unpleasant experience for her depends on how she interprets Bob's actions. She could think, 'He did that so gently, it's as if he read my mind', or she could think, 'How dare he fondle my breasts without asking first'. Can you understand that whether it feels good or bad for Lisa has more to do with how she interprets Bob's actions than it does with the physical act of touching her intimately?

Lisa may have religious beliefs that taught her that sex before marriage is a sin. Like many young people, she may say that she has rejected those beliefs, yet they could still be having a profound effect on her attitudes to sexual intimacy. She could feel guilty without understanding the origin of that feeling. How you feel when you are intimate depends on what is going on inside you – your internal reality. A guy can kiss a girl he really likes and it's a brilliant experience for him. He feels really great afterwards – alive, and so happy that he wants to skip. Later that evening, he is with another girl who is out for a good time. They have sex and it's an anticlimax. He enjoys the few moments of physical pleasure and afterwards he feels empty. There is a lack of ease in him that makes him feel disconnected.

When men feel down, they tend to go off and do something physical to distract themselves. Women are more likely to take time out to sit with their feelings and see if they can find out why they feel as they do. Outside of surveys that are done for research, young people rarely admit publicly that sex leaves them unfulfilled. Yet the problem pages of magazines are packed with letters from disillusioned lovers who are unhappy and looking for advice on what they need to do to find the satisfaction they desire.

There are as many reasons for unsatisfactory sex as there are people who are afraid to be honest. The same action can be a turn-on when you are with one person, and with a different person a horribly negative experience. Even with the same partner, it can be a turn-on at one time and leave you cold at another. Why? The difference is not in the partner or partners, it's in you. Your response is different because your thinking has changed. The same physically intimate actions feel different because your response to the meaning those actions have for you is different every time.

Physical feelings are very important when a couple have sex, but they are only one part of lovemaking. How a person responds physically to sex involves the whole person: body, emotions and spirit. Let me define the physical as the bodily sensations, the emotional as the feeling response to how one thinks and interprets, and the spiritual as the deeper awareness of who you are and how connected you are to the self and the other. In its wider meaning, spirituality is also related to how you connect to creation, nature, the universe, or God. How you respond spiritually takes you within, to that interior space where you are in touch with the sacred self. Another way of putting it is that sex is really great when two become one and there is a meeting of souls. Religion is meant to lead to spirituality, but frequently it doesn't. It's poor religious teaching that creates that association between sex and guilt.

Love Needs Commitment

I believe that a basic human instinct for a couple who fall in love is to want a monogamous relationship. Hardly anyone can fall in love with someone and feel that it is OK for them to date other people. Being in love makes it easier to be faithful because the love drug PEA heightens awareness of the beloved, and in contrast, others seem to look less attractive and desirable.

When women are in a sexual relationship, they are more likely than men to want it to be monogamous and to seek a long-term commitment. For many, this means marriage, and for a growing number of couples, it means moving in to live together. In the very recent past, many couples had sex with only one partner – the person they married. Today that is changing, and serial monogamy, where a person is faithful to a partner when they are in a relationship, but when that ends, moves on and has a faithful relationship with another partner, is becoming very common.

Attitudes have changed radically and there is a widespread acceptance of premarital sex in our society. Many couples who are in a committed relationship fail to recognise that they may still need to practise 'safe sex'. It is estimated that one in five sexually active people in the United States has a sexual disease. Many couples in a long-term relationship stop using protection because they believe they are sexually safe. If either person has had previous partners, they may be at risk.

A sexual encounter can be a wonderfully spiritual, bonding experience between two people who are in love and desire to give of themselves at the deepest possible level – and it can appear to be all of those things and still turn out to be a disaster. We all know people who believed they were in a stable relationship only to discover that their partner is cheating. Immediately, the meaning of the relationship changes and instead of feeling loved and connected, the innocent party feels devastated by how cruelly they have been conned.

Couples who enjoy erotic, passionate, sensuous sex are communicating beyond words in a way that excites, energises and bonds spiritually with a love energy that leaves each partner feeling valued and special. It's hardly surprising that studies show that people who are in exclusive, committed relationships report the greatest satisfaction with their love lives.

After about eighteen months, the intoxication of the love drug PEA wears off and is replaced by another drug. The body produces endorphins – soothing substances that make us feel warm and content and peaceful. These don't wear off. The longer one stays in a relationship and the happier one is, the more endorphins are released. It takes time to get to know a partner and build the kind of trusting relationship where you feel free to be yourself. Studies show that people feel more intimate when partners see them as they see themselves rather than idealise them.

Disempowering Sex

A sexual encounter without any emotional involvement is disempowering. It is because of its potential to cause hurt at a very deep level that religious teaching says it is a sin, a failure to show love. When a person uses another sexually, their intention may just be to have a good time. We all know that some young people go out at the weekend to have 'a few drinks and a shag'. They see nothing wrong with setting out to find a like-minded partner who will have sex, with no strings attached. I meet students regularly who claim to be happy to 'get their little bit on the side'. I also meet those who were deeply hurt by casual sex and didn't realise how they were emotionally damaged until months, or even years later.

Sex without love is a selfish act that breeds loneliness and dissatisfaction. The devastation of a teenage girl who finds that the guy with whom she had sex has no feelings for her is a very painful life lesson. Sadly, many young women fail to learn from experience and recreate the same kind of painful experience with partner after partner. They are looking for love and the truth is they have such a distorted idea of what love is that they are willing to settle for a brief sexual interlude in the hope that this time they will get the love and esteem they want. They never do, because looking to others to make you feel good simply doesn't work.

Men and women who have sex with different partners always have self-esteem issues to be resolved. When you value yourself, you will not allow others to treat you badly or to use you sexually. Your sacred self knows that you deserve better. We all make mistakes in life, and if one partner fails to treat you well, learn from the experience. If it happens again, you have yet to learn the lesson. You need to take responsibility for the choices you make. You hurt yourself when you settle for less than you deserve.

Women are warned regularly against men who are only out for one thing. It's clear that a woman who has sex to entice a guy to stay with her needs to learn how to value her own sacred self. It's equally true, but not so publicly acknowledged, that guys also get used sexually. Men also look for love, and enormous damage is done to the ego of the man who is seduced and left. Historically, it has been the practice for a man to feel OK when he was sexually involved with a woman and not feeling anything. Sexual equality has turned the tables and often it is only when a man finds out that his partner has no more feelings for him than he has for her that he experiences a huge let-down, a sense of being used and discarded that is damaging to self-esteem and self-image.

When either a man or woman uses another person by sexually exploiting them, both suffer. This applies whether we are talking about two ten-year-olds intimately kissing for a dare or a sixteen-year-old going out to have sex with any girl who proves willing because all his friends are boasting that they have 'done it', or a lonely single who wants to wake up in the morning with someone beside them.

When there is no commitment to the other, the sense of caring that is necessary for satisfying sex is absent, so what you have is two people with high expectations of sex that will not be fulfilled. When people engage in sexual activity, what they really want is to feel intimate – close to someone who makes them feel good about themselves. We all want to feel loved for who we are, and I hardly need to spell it out. No man or woman will have this need met in a relationship where they feel used to give sexual release.

Does Practice Make Perfect?

Our society is failing to educate young people about what is really involved in having a wonderful sexual relationship. They learn about 'safe sex', but not about honest communication. Britain has the highest rate of unmarried pregnancy in the world. Sex for the vast majority of sexually active teenagers is a disaster, and not at all like the pleasurable and fulfilling experiences that people brag about. Writing in the *Australian National Times,* Adele Horin gives an excellent description of teenage sex. 'For teenage boys with racing hormones, the process of intercourse is quick and explosive: an awesome, out-of-control rush to orgasm. It will never be as quick or driven at any other time in their lives. For many young girls, the rip-roaring intercourse is a terrible disappointment.'

A young man who wants to be a sensitive lover has to train himself to delay his orgasm until his partner is ready. This will not happen unless he is aware of the emotional needs of his partner. The natural male instinct is for orgasm and the ejaculation of sperm. A male has a strong biological urge to plant his seed widely to ensure procreation and reproduction of the species. In order for him to humanise that instinct and discover the intimacy of a relationship – the tenderness, mutuality and reciprocity required of a sensitive lover – he needs to be taught about both male and female sexual responsiveness. He also needs the communication skills to talk to her and find out what she enjoys with a partner.

Where sex is concerned with only the physical, practice rarely makes perfect. The teenage boy who is an insensitive lover has not learned that a woman's body is slower to respond sexually than a man's. Unless he reads a book like this, he may never find out. Men assume women are sexually satisfied. Even when a partner or spouse trusts a man enough to suggest something to make lovemaking a better experience, some men may not accede to the request.

In counselling, many couples admit to knowing that each partner's needs were not being met, but feeling that they could not discuss the problem. How helpful is it for a man to be told that he needs to develop the self-discipline to delay his own pleasure until his partner is sufficiently aroused? How can a young man find out what that means in practice? Men have heard that foreplay is necessary to turn on a woman, but when they are asked specifically what kind of foreplay women like, they nearly always focus on the physical. This is hardly surprising.

So much sexual pleasure is personal, and what pleases one woman may not meet the needs of another.

I tell my students that every satisfying and fulfilling sexual encounter begins with foreplay, and the first step in foreplay is talking. Any couple who focuses on the physical and fails to pay attention to the emotions and spirituality of the other is missing out, and whether they are consciously aware of it or not, they will have unmet needs.

It's surprising how many men are scared about communication and feel they lack the ability to talk to a woman. It doesn't have to be a deeply intimate discussion. Most women feel close when they talk about the ordinary everyday things that happen to the people who are important in their lives. Talking helps them feel connected and this creates the sense of intimacy that a woman needs to open up sexually. The communication that leads to bonding with a woman is so simple that one can become proficient after just a little practice.

Step 1 Let her talk and listen
Step 2 Identify how you think she is feeling
Step 3 Put what you heard in Step 1 into your own words - this is called reflective listening - and add, 'It sounds like you're feeling —' happy, depressed, angry, excited or whatever feeling you think. That's all there is to it!

Let's say Danny meets Mary after work. She begins to tell him what a terrible day she has had. Danny can see that she is tired and depressed so he says something like, 'You've had a dreadful day. It sounds like you feel tired and depressed.' Danny has made the connection that will make Mary feel he hears her and understands how she feels.

Loving communication does not judge or blame. It never condemns or puts the other down and is always gentle with the truth.

RECREATIONAL SEX

In our society, sex is used to advertise every kind of product and whether we like to admit it or not this makes sex a commodity. People are influenced by what they see on television. One result of being surrounded by sexy advertising is that there is an overt message that it's OK to use sex for material gain. It's only a tiny little step away from this to accepting it's OK to use sex as a commodity that makes you feel good. Advertising fosters the belief that it's OK for big business to exploit sex for commercial gain so why should the ordinary punter not exploit others sexually for personal satisfaction?

The beautiful, sexy people who are used to advertise products on television create expectations that make people feel dissatisfied with their less than perfect bodies. The advertisers cleverly suggest to us that if only we use their products we will become more attractive, smell better, have more status and be readily identified as popular. They help to perpetuate the myth that external forces make us feel any or all of these things.

Our society teaches us to look outside ourselves to get our physical and emotional needs met. We learn that variety is the spice of life, so there is a whole industry out there, taking money for showing us how to make our relationships and our sex lives more exciting. The focus is mainly on the physical aspects of sex, and although some do emphasise the need for an emotional connection, few, if any, give any importance to the spirituality of sex.

We have seen that sexual desire has more to do with the brain than the body and that wrong information about sex and relationships spreads like noxious weeds that keep changing and adapting to survive. The pre-teenage girl is sexually attracted to a boy and her friends arrange for them to meet. When he tries to kiss her she feels frightened and excited, embarrassed and thrilled. Yet when she talks to her friends, she leaves out the not-so-good parts. Many kids lie when kissing is not a good experience because they don't want to admit to their friends that they didn't really enjoy it.

In those situations girls tend to think there is something wrong with them – that they didn't get it right. Boys are more likely to think that the girl has a problem and set out to find a partner who is a better kisser. Older teenagers with a little experience read books and magazines that explain how to spice up your love life or your one-night stand.

The *Cosmopolitan* booklet on *1,000 All Time, Best-Ever Sex Tips, Tricks and Techniques suggests:* 'Use a vanilla-scented lip gloss, then move up close – the soft aroma is guaranteed to get him to kiss you. No time for a shower – get him to lick you clean. Send him a nicely wrapped box with a vacuum bag inside and scrawl on it that you're going to put the vacuum cleaner to shame tonight. Give him a present of erotic lingerie for you'.

I find these suggestions hilarious, but the tragedy is that many people take them seriously, and when they try them out and they don't result in amazingly erotic pleasure, they blame their own lack of whatever. Companies will not spend money on products that don't sell and if you give even the most cursory look around you in a magazine store, magazines with sex tips are hot sellers.

However, there are positive signs of change. There is an article in an issue of Oprah Winfrey's magazine *O*, about why twenty-four million women don't want sex. Writer Audrey Edwards quotes from author and counsellor Gwendolyn Goldsby Grant's book *The Best Kind of Loving*. She explains, 'A man's sexuality is ever present and available to him – he can see it and hold it in his hand. He's programmed for quick arousal. A woman's arousal is more in her spirit than in her body. Unless you get to her spirit, you haven't gotten to her sexually.'

The spirituality of sexuality is the key to uncovering the element that is missing when people feel a lack of satisfaction with sex. I meet people all the time who would like me to forbid young people to have sex and demand that I speak out against young adults who cohabit. They fail to understand that anyone who forbids adolescents to experiment sexually is wasting their breath. A much more respectful way of encouraging young people to delay getting sexually involved prematurely is to give them the kind of clear, accurate information they need.

Body, Mind and Spirit

I cannot make decisions for anyone else. If I demand that others change their behaviour or actions, I am telling them what to do. I am failing to respect their right to make their own decisions. You are the only person who knows if you are ready to have sex, although I respectfully suggest that this is not the question that you need to answer. A more helpful way to make a decision may be to acknowledge that there are many different parts in you that affect any decision you make to have sex.

Where sex is concerned, the body may be crying out for physical intimacy and the brain opposing it. She meets a guy who is drop-dead gorgeous and her body says, 'Let's have sex' and her brain says, 'He'll love you and leave you.' Enjoying physical pleasure is at the surface level. You can have sexual thrills without emotional involvement, but the brain plays an important role in how good the sexy feelings are. Emotional involvement is necessary for sex to feel fulfilling.

Almost everyone accepts that physical and emotional involvement is essential for intimate sex. It's surprising how many people think the spiritual connection which brings one to the deepest level of intimacy is unimportant. When spirituality is ignored, how can you see the fantasies you believe for what they are? How can you drop the illusions of finding the perfect partner unless you are aware that what you seek is within you? In the absence of that spiritual dimension, you will continue to look externally, to find someone to fulfil your needs, and while you do this, you will always have expectations of how the other should be, and how you should be. No matter how realistic or how wonderful your expectations are, they will get in the way, because they will act like barriers in your brain that will stop you fully entering into the experience of sexual intimacy.

When expectations make a person focus on how they think sex should be they cannot enjoy it as it is – they have to compare it to their fantasy of how it should be. You know that great sex has far more to do with what is happening in the brain than in the genitals. It's only when you make the spiritual connection that you understand how to drop all the expectations you hold about how you or your partner should be. It's only when you have that sense of self-acceptance that brings you to revere the sacred self that you are free to let go of any anxiety about body shape, about being too fat or too thin or having the wrong size breasts or not having a six-pack. Now you are ready for the healthy relationship that allows you the freedom to be who you are. As Kahlil Gibran wrote in *The Prophet*:

> *Love one another but make not a bond of love;*
> *Let it rather be a moving sea between the shores of your souls.*
> *Fill each other's cup but drink not from one cup.*
> *Give one another of your bread but eat not from the same loaf.*
> *Sing and dance together and be joyous, but let each one of you be alone.*

This is the dream relationship that breeds the freedom which allows you to be totally relaxed, to let go of your control and give yourself over fully to enter into the experience without any expectations. This love is nurtured in the awareness of the sacred self that reaches out in love to others. May you experience it some day.

BIBLIOGRAPHY

Books

Adler, Alfred. *The Sexual Function: Superiority and Social Interests.* Evanstown, North-Western University Press, 1964.

Andreas, Dr Connierae and Steve Andreas. *Heart of the Mind.* Moab, Utah, Real People Press, 1989.

Bass, Ellen and Laura Davis. *The Courage to Heal.* New York, Cedar, 1994.

Bausch, William J. *Becoming a Man.* Connecticut, Twenty-Third Publications, 1988.

Bennett, Dr David. *Growing Pains.* Northamptonshire, Thorsons, 1987.

Berne, Eric. *Games People Play: The Psychology of Human Relationships.* Harmondsworth, Penguin, 1969.

Best Ron, Peter Lang, Caroline Lodge, Chris Watkins. *Pastoral Care and Personal Social Education.* London, Cassell, 1995.

Block, Joel D. *Secrets of Better Sex.* New York, Parker Publishing, 1996.

Bloom, Allen. *Love and Friendship.* New York, Touchstone, 1993.

Bradshaw, John. *Family Secrets.* New York, Bantam, 1995.

Bradshaw, John. *Homecoming.* London, Piatkus, 1999.

Bradshaw, John. *Healing the Shame that Binds You.* Florida, HCI, 1988.

Bradshaw, John. *The Family.* Florida, HCI, 1988.

Catechism of the Catholic Church, Dublin, Veritas, 1994.

Clarke, Keith. *An Experience of Celibacy.* Notre Dame, Ave Maria Press, 1982.

Cline, Sally. *Lifting the Taboo.* London, Little, Brown, 1995.

Cline, Sally. *Couples.* London, Little, Brown, 1998.

Clulow, Christopher. *Women, Men and Marriage: Talks from the Tavistock Marital Studies Institute.* London, Sheldon Press, 1995.

Collins, Pat. *Intimacy and the Hungers of the Heart.* Dublin, Columba Press, 1991.

Cox, Tracey. *Hot Relationships – How to Have One.* London, Corgi, 1999.

De Mello, Anthony. *Awareness.* London, Fount Paperbacks, 1990.

De Mello, Anthony. *Walking on Water.* Dublin, Columba Press, 1998.

Dickson, Anne. *The Mirror Within: A New Look at Sexuality.* London, Quartet Books, 1987.

Dillon, Valerie Vance. *Becoming a Woman.* Dublin, Columba, 1991.

Dominion, Jack. *An Introduction to Marital Problems.* London, Fount Paperbacks, 1986.

Forward, Susan. *Toxic Parents.* New York, Bantam Books, 1990.

Frankl, Viktor. *Man's Search for Meaning.* New York, Washington Square Press, 1965.

Gaffney, Maureen. *The Way We Live Now.* Dublin, Gill and Macmillan, 1996.

Gathorne-Hardy, Jonathan. *Sex: the Measure of All Things – a Life of A. Kinsey.* London, Chatto & Windus, 1998.

Gibran, Kahlil. *The Prophet*. Oxford, Oneworld, 1995.
Gleitman, Henry, Alan J. Fridlund, Daniel Reisberg. *Psychology*. New York, Norton, 1999 (Fifth Edition).
Goergen, Donald. *The Sexual Celibate*. London, SPCK, 1976.
Goleman, Daniel. *Emotional Intelligence*. London, Bloomsbury, 1996.
Gray, Anthony. *Speaking of Sex*. London, Cassell, 1993.
Gray, John. *Men Are from Mars, Women Are from Venus*. London, Thorsons, 1993.
Herron, Aidan and Dominic McGinley. *Tell Them*. Dublin, Mentor Publications, 1987.
Humphreys, Tony. *Myself, My Partner*. Dublin, Gill and Macmillan, 1997.
Humphreys, Tony. *Self-Esteem: The Key to Your Child's Education*. Middleton, Carrig Print, 1993.
Hite, Shere. *The New Hite Report*. London, Hamlyn, 2000.
Inglis, Tom. *Lessons in Irish Sexuality*. Dublin, UCD, 1998.
Kilroy, Patricia,. *If Your Child Is Gay or Lesbian*. Parents' Support, Gay Switchboard, Dublin, 2000.
Kinsey, Alfred. *The Sexual Behaviour in the Human Male*. Philadelphia, W. B. Saunders Co., 1948.
Kinsey, Alfred. *The Sexual Behaviour in the Human Female*. Philadelphia, W. B. Saunders Co., 1953.
Kohner, Nancy. *What Shall We Tell The Children*. London, BBC Books, 1993.
Kramer, Dr Jonathan and Diane Dunaway. *Why Men Don't Get Enough Sex and Women Love*. London, Virgin Books, 1994.
Lawson, Michael. *The Better Marriage Guide*. London, Hodder and Stoughton, 1998.
Low, Dr Lynne. *Understanding Sex*. Thelford, Family Doctor Series, 1997.
MacNamara, Angela. *Ready Steady Grow*. Dublin, Veritas Publications, 1991.
Margolies, Eva. *Undressing the American Male*. New York, Dutton, 1995.
Masters W., V. Johnson and R. Kolodny. *Human Sexuality*. New York, Norton, 1995.
May, Rollo. *Freedom and Destiny*. New York, Norton, 1998.
McDonnell, Albert. *When Strangers Marry: a Study of Marriage Breakdown in Ireland*. Dublin, Columba Press, 1999.
McDowell, Josh. *Why Say No to Sex?* Eastbourne, Kingsway Publications, 1990.
McHugh, Richard. *Mind with a Heart: Creative Patterns of Personal Change*. Gujarat Sahitya Prakash, 1999.
Mussen, Paul Henry et al. *Child Development and Personality*. New York, Harper and Row, 1984.
National Marriage Guidance Council. *Sex Education in Perspective: A Symposium on Work in Progress*. Rugby, 1972.

Nelson, Richard. *Human Relationship Skills, Training and Self Help*. London, Cassell, 1990.

Orbach, Susie. *The Impossibility of Sex*. London, Penguin, 2000.

Pearsall, Dr Paul. *Super Marital Sex: An Important New Study of Sexuality*. London, Ebury Press, 1988.

Pease, Alan and Barbara. *Why Men Don't Listen and Women Can't Read Maps*. Victoria, Harper Collins, 1999.

Pickering, Lucienne. *Boy Talk*. London, Geoffrey Chapman, 1992.

Pickering, Lucienne. *Girl Talk*. London, Geoffrey Chapman, 1992.

Powell, Elizabeth. *Talking Back to Sexual Pressure*. Minnesota, Compcare Publishers, 1991.

Powell, John. *The Secret of Staying in Love*. Allen, Texas, Thomas More, 1974.

Powell, John. *Unconditional Love*. Allen, Texas, Thomas More, 1978.

Powell, John. *Why Am I Afraid to Love*. Allen, Texas, Thomas More, 1967.

Powell, John. *Happiness Is an Inside Job*. Allen, Texas, Thomas More, 1989.

Powell, John. *Fully Human, Fully Alive*. Allen, Texas, Thomas More, 1976.

Powell, John. *Why Am I Afraid to Tell You Who I Am?* Allen, Texas, Thomas More, 1969.

Powell, John and Loretta Brady. *Will the Real Me Please Stand Up*. Allen, Texas, Thomas More, 1985.

Prior, Robert and Joseph O'Connor. *Neuro-Linguistic Programming and Relationships*. London, Thorsons, 2000.

Quinn, Michal and Terri. *What Can a Parent Do?* Dublin, Veritas, 1986.

Quinn, Michal and Terri. *Parenting and Sex*. Newry, Family Caring Trust, 1991.

Reinhold, Dr Margaret. *How to Survive in Spite of Your Parents*. London, Cedar, 1999.

Reinisch, June with Ruth Beasley. *The Kinsey Institute New Report on Sex*. New York, St Martin's Press, 1990.

Rosenthal, Don and Martha. *Intimacy: The Noble Adventure*. Cork, Collins Press, 1999.

Satir, Virginia. *Peoplemaking*. Palo Alto, Science and Behaviour Books, 1972.

Shalit, Wendy. *A Return to Modesty*. New York, Free Press, 1999.

Sheehy, Gail. *New Passages*. London, Harper Collins, 1996.

Silin, Jonathan G. Sex, Death and the Education of Children. New York, Teachers' College Press, 1995.

Skynner, Robin and John Cleese. *Life and How to Survive It*. London, Vermilion, 1993.

Skynner, Robin and John Cleese. *Families and How to Survive Them*. London, Mandarin, 1989.

Smith, Anthony. *The Human Body*. London, BBC Books, 1998.

Spock, Dr Benjamin. *Bringing Children Up in a Difficult Time*. London, New English Library, 1977.

St Clair, Miriam T. *The Vice of Today.* Limerick, City Printing Company, 1992.
Tannen, Deborah. *That's Not What I Meant.* London, Virago, 1992.
Tannen, Deborah. *You Just Don't Understand.* London, Virago, 1992.
Valles, Carlos G. *Courage to Be Myself.* Gujarat Sahitya Prakash, 1991.
Van Breemen, Peter G. *As Bread that is Broken.* New Jersey, Dimension Books, 1974.
Vanzant, Iyanla. *In the Meantime.* London, Pocket Books, 1998.
Walker, Richard. *Sex and Relationships: The Complete Family Guide.* London, De Agostini, 1996.
Wardlaw, Carole. *One in Every Family.* Dublin, Basement Press, 1994.
Westheimer, Dr Ruth K. *Sex for Dummies.* Foster City, IDG Books, 1995.
Whitehead, Evelyn Eaton and James D. *A Sense of Sexuality.* New York, First Image Books, 1990.
Wynne, Carmel. *Relationships and Sexuality.* Dublin, Mercier Press, 1997.

Articles in Newspapers, Magazine and Journals

Andrews, Paul. 'The Tasks and Pitfalls of Growing Up'. *Studies*, 81, 324, Winter 1992

Argyle, M. et al. 'The Communication of Inferior and Superior Attitudes by Verbal and Non-verbal Signals'. *British Journal of Social and Clinical Psychology*, 9, Part 3, September 1970

Coldrey, Barry. 'The Sexual Abuse of Children'. *Studies*, 85, 240, Winter 1996

Gaffney, Maureen. 'Adolescence and Family Conflict'. *Studies*, 81, 324, Winter 1992

Miller, B. C. and K. A. Moore. 'Adolescent Sexual Behaviour, Pregnancy and Parenting: Research Through the 1990s'. *Journal of Marriage and the Family*, 52, 1024-44

Magazines
B. PPA.
Bliss. Emap-élan
Cosmopolitan. The National Magazine Company Ltd.
Face Up. Redemptorist Publications.
J17. Emap-élan.
Marie Claire. IPC.
Miz. IPC.
More. Emap-élan.
New Woman. Emap-élan.
O, the Oprah Magazine
Playboy. Playboy Publications.
Sugar. PPA.